DESCRIPTIVE CATALOGING OF RARE BOOKS

Second Edition

Webster University LIBRARY

Cataloging Distribution Service, Library of Congress
Washington, D.C. 1991

A revision of the edition published in 1981 under title: Bibliographic Description of Rare Books

Prepared by a working group under the auspices of:

      Office for Descriptive Cataloging Policy
          Library of Congress
     and
      Bibliographic Standards Committee of the
          Rare Books and Manuscripts Section
          Association of College and Research Libraries
          American Library Association

Library of Congress Cataloging-in-Publication Data

Descriptive Cataloging of rare books.—2nd ed.
    p. cm.
  Rev. ed. of: Bibliographic description of rare books. 1981.
  "Prepared by a working group under the auspices of Office for Descriptive Cataloging Policy, Library of Congress and Bibliographic Standards Committee of the Rare Books and Manuscripts Section, Association of College and Research Libraries, American Library Association."—T.p. verso.
  ISBN 0-8444-0690-2
  1. Cataloging of rare books—Rules. 2. Rare books—Bibliography—Methodology. 3. Anglo-American cataloging rules. 4. Descriptive cataloging—Rules. I. Library of Congress. Office for Descriptive Cataloging Policy. II. Association of College and Research Libraries. Rare Books and Manuscripts Section. Bibliographic Standards Committee. III. Library of Congress. Office for Descriptive Cataloging Policy. Bibliographic description of rare books.
  Z695.74.U54 1991
  025.3'416—dc20
                                            91-6988
                                              CIP

TABLE OF CONTENTS

PREFACE TO THE SECOND EDITION

The Background

In 1981 the Library of Congress published *Bibliographic Description of Rare Books* (BDRB), a manual of rules designed primarily for its own catalogers, but also intended to respond to the expressed needs of those outside the Library who catalog rare materials. The Library considers the manual to have been one of its most successful efforts in taking care of specialized cataloging requirements. Nevertheless, in the ten years since catalogers began applying the rules, a growing body of experience, research, and discussion made it increasingly clear that eventually some changes and additions to the rules would be needed. Then, in early 1989, because the Library of Congress was near to exhausting its stock of copies for sale, it had to decide what to do about reprinting or revising BDRB. The circulation of drafts of a revised edition of *ISBD(A): International Standard Bibliographic Description for Older Monographic Publications (Antiquarian)* near the same time was also a catalyst, stimulating the interest of the Bibliographic Standards Committee of the Rare Books and Manuscripts Section of the Association of College and Research Libraries in helping to prepare a new edition of BDRB. Discussions between the representatives of the Committee and of the Library were positive, and from that point, progress was rapid.

A timetable was agreed upon for circulating two revised drafts of the rules during 1990 and for issuing the second edition of the rules early in 1991. The Committee solicited widespread participation from colleagues in the United States and abroad, prepared numerous discussion papers, and held open discussions at three American Library Association conferences (June 1989, January 1990, and June 1990). A final editorial meeting of representatives from the Committee and the Library was held at the Library of Congress in November 1990.

This Edition

The second edition of these rules for rare materials brings the 1981 version up to date in the following ways:

1. **Title change**. This was done because there appears to be general agreement that the phrase "bibliographic description" is too suggestive of traditional descriptive bibliography. To avoid confusion and make it quite clear that the rules are for library catalogers rather than bibliographers, the words "bibliographic description" have been replaced by "descriptive cataloging." This phrase is also more appropriate because the text now includes some advice on access points, which in library parlance cannot be said to be covered by "bibliographic description."

2. **Cosmetic improvements**. A number of changes have been made in order to correct typographical and other obvious errors, and to make improvements in wording that have been the fruit of ten years of catalogers' experience with BDRB. These alterations will not require changes in catalog records that were produced under BDRB. Rather, it is hoped that they will make DCRB easier to read and interpret, and thereby promote a more consistent application of the rules.

3. **Substantive changes**. Some of the changes made in this new edition will result in varying degrees of difference between BDRB and DCRB records. It should be noted that some of these changes are actually due to changes found in the 1988 Revision of the Anglo-American Cataloguing Rules, Second Edition (cf. the change noted below under point m). A summary of the more important changes follows:

a. Clarified and simplified options for recording punctuation; similarly improved instructions for using the mark of omission (rule 0E)

b. Rewritten instructions for transcribing early letter forms (rule 0H)

c. Changed wording to allow more latitude in determining which types of information may be omitted from the title and responsibility area, with or without using the mark of omission (rule 1A2)

d. Clarified instructions for recording data from the title page (rule 1A2) and particularly for recording the title proper (rule 1B1-1B3); with a new definition of "title page" added to the Glossary

e. The possibility of the use of caption titles beyond single-sheet publications made explicit in the rewritten rule 1B3

f. Various changes in the recording of other title information (rule 1D), including a new provision allowing for such statements as "in two volumes" (rule 1D3)

g. Notes regarding transposition of elements within the title and statement of responsibility area made mandatory (e.g., rule 1B1 or 1G3)

h. Several changes in the rules for recording complex publisher statements (e.g., rule 4C6)

i. New provisions for transcribing words and phrases such as "printed in the year" or "anno" in the publication, etc. area (cf. rules for area 4)

j. Changed instructions for recording date of impression (rule 4E)

k. Clarified instructions for recording unnumbered leaves in the statement of extent, and the provision for disjunct unnumbered errata leaves changed to include them in the statement of extent (rules 5B3, 5B4)

l. Clarified provisions for giving sizes of single sheets (rule 5D5)

m. Revised rules for accompanying material (rule 5E), and the elimination of rule 9 (due specifically to changes in AACR 2)

n. Examples of notes illustrating the provisions of area 7 modified to delete prescribed punctuation, except for 7C16 and 7C19

o. Expanded provisions for noting statements of responsibility (rule 7C6)

p. Provisions for the "With:" note expanded and clarified (rule 7C19)

4. **New options**. Two new options have been added, which when implemented will result in further differences between BDRB and DCRB records:

    a. An option allowing a note for the full collational formula, instead of a simple signature note (rule 7C9)

    b. An option allowing the "fingerprint" to be recorded (rule 8)

5. **Works cited**. A bibliography based on citations found within the rules has been compiled to assist catalogers in identifying other publications useful in the cataloging of rare books and special collections.

6. **Appendices**. The appendices in the first edition were limited to examples and a glossary. The glossary (Appendix G) has been retained and expanded, and to this second edition have been added the following:

Appendix A for "Title Access Points": some advice for additional access by title that might be consider "extra" in routine library cataloging

Appendix B for "Early Letter Forms": background information for the proper application of rule 0H, which gives brief instructions for transcribing with some adjustment the obsolete forms of letters and diacritical marks typically found in books printed before modern times

Appendix C for "Rare Serials": a CONSER-approved reformulation of the guidelines for cataloging rare serials that were published in *Cataloging Service Bulletin*, no. 26 (fall 1984)

Appendix D for "Minimal-Level Records": instructions for preparing less-than-full cataloging in a manner that adequately identifies rare materials

Appendix E for "DCRB Code for Records": an explanation, with instructions, for all the situations in which subfield ǂe of USMARC field 040 is appropriate as an indication of the application of the present set of rules (It should be noted that the Library of Congress has changed the code "bdrb" to "dcrb.")

Appendix F for "Concordance between Rules in DCRB and AACR 2": a concordance relating the rules in AACR 2 to those in the present set of rules

It will be noted that the previous appendix composed of ten full-record examples has been dropped. Although there have been many requests for more examples (either to be included in the text or appended at the end), the labor that would be required to select and verify them, and then provide for their clear and careful reproduction, appeared to be more than the Library or the Committee felt they could undertake without a much larger commitment of time and human resources than was available. A compendium of examples to supplement DCRB therefore remains as a *desideratum*.

7. **Index**. An index has been added in response to numerous requests.

DCRB, ISBD(A), and AACR 2

In updating the 1981 text we duly considered the final draft text of the second edition of ISBD(A), and tried as much as possible to conform to it. Still, this second edition must perforce — as is true of all cataloging done at the Library — remain generally in harmony with the parent code of cataloging rules, AACR 2, and in consequence, where there is a substantial difference between AACR 2 and ISBD stipulations, DCRB usually follows AACR 2 rather than ISBD(A). A good example of this would be the rule for the prescribed source for the edition area, which is limited to the title page in ISBD(A), while both AACR 2 and DCRB prescribe the title page, preliminaries, and colophon for this area. In other cases, DCRB is now in harmony with ISBD(A) (cf., for example, the new provision in 4D1 for recording words and phrases associated with the date element). Another category of essential differences between ISBD(A) and DCRB derives from the fact that DCRB, which is a body of cataloging rules, treats many subjects in considerably greater detail than does the international standard for rare books. The treatment of early letter forms in transcription, the specifications for caption titles and for single-sheet publications represent prominent examples of this difference between the rules and the standard for rare books. On the other hand, given the inclusion of at least some detailed stipulations in the standard which make it resemble cataloging rules, it is useful to make a clear distinction between ISBD(A) and DCRB, at least within the United States. With DCRB we have cataloging rules covering all the materials covered by ISBD(A), and there is then no competition between standards and rules. Our daily operation as we do the work of cataloging in each institution means applying our rules, not the standards. This does not mean that we have no need for the standards. As already suggested, ISBD(A) represents an international standard to be considered as one of our source documents when we come to write or rewrite cataloging rules for rare materials.

Any competition that remains might be said to lie between DCRB and AACR 2 rules 2.12-2.18. Libraries with few rare materials may prefer to follow AACR 2, including rules 2.12-2.18, without regard for DCRB. The Library of Congress disregards rules 2.12-2.18 altogether, applying instead their amplified counterparts in DCRB (cf. the concordance in Appendix F).

Acknowledgments

This second edition was prepared as a collaborative effort of the ACRL RBMS Bibliographic Standards Committee and the Library of Congress. The chief coordinators of the effort were Jackie M. Dooley, acting in her capacity as chairperson of the Committee, and Ben R. Tucker, with the generous assistance of Robert B. Ewald, representing the Library of Congress.

Other members of the Committee during the work on the revision were Sidney Berger, Virginia Bartow, Scott Carlisle, Eve Pasternak, Deborah Ryszka, Cynthia Shelton, Joe Springer, Laura Stalker, M. Susan Taraba, and Belinda D. Urquiza. Additional RBMS members who assisted in the review were John Attig, Bonnie Dede, Alan Degutis, Mollie Della Terza, Elizabeth Herman, Elizabeth Johnson, Sara Shatford Layne, Alexandra Mason, Janice Matthiesen, Hope Mayo, Patrick Russell, and John Thomas.

In addition to serving on the Committee, Belinda D. Urquiza of the Library of Congress coordinated mailings and compiled all the comments with heroic efficiency. She was ably assisted by Library of Congress rare book catalogers Roger J. Trienens and Matthew Caulfield in reviewing all comments in detail and drafting rule revisions. The John Carter Brown Library kindly permitted David Rich to revise his index, originally published in 1987 under the copyright of the John Carter Brown Library, and allowed its publication as an integral part of this edition of DCRB.

Scores of rare book catalogers in the United States and abroad took the time to comment on the earlier BDRB rules and on the two draft revisions. All of these comments were scrutinized and evaluated, and many contributors will find their suggestions reflected in the final text. To everyone who participated, we extend thanks for a very gratifying collaborative effort, one which it is fervently hoped will be useful to all catalogers of rare materials.

A final special note of thanks is due Mary Lou Miller of the Automation Planning and Liaison Office of the Library of Congress, who planned and then managed the printing of both the second draft and the final camera-ready copy. Her generous contribution of time and expertise while working under other deadlines is deeply appreciated.

Jackie M. Dooley
RBMS Bibliographic Standards Committee (ALA/ACRL)

Ben R. Tucker
Chief, Office for Descriptive Cataloging Policy
Library of Congress

PREFACE TO THE 1981 EDITION

As rare book catalogers and librarians began in 1977 and 1978 to make preparations for the adoption of the second edition of the *Anglo-American Cataloguing Rules* (AACR 2), it became apparent that the code's brief section on rare printed materials at the end of its second chapter might benefit from some expansion and elaboration to address in a more complete way the often troublesome questions of rare book description. A comparable reaction to the general provisions of ISBD(G) had already prompted the formation of a special working group within the International Federation of Library Associations and Institutions (IFLA), which had as its goal the preparation of a complementary ISBD that might form the basis for international practice in the description of older materials.

Near the end of 1977, just as work was being completed on AACR 2, the first draft of *ISBD(A): International Standard Bibliographic Description for Older Books (Antiquarian)*[1] was issued, and a few of its initial provisions were actually incorporated into AACR 2. It was not possible, however, to delay the publication schedule of AACR 2 while this and other ISBD work progressed toward conclusion. As the IFLA Working Group on ISBD(A) (under the guidance of Richard Christophers, British Library) issued succeeding drafts in 1978 and 1979, the Library of Congress and other rare book cataloging agencies in the United States watched the progress of the text with increasing interest, and many institutional and individual responses to the drafts were prepared and forwarded to the Working Group.

The need to have a single cataloging standard, based on AACR 2 but approaching the cataloging of rare materials with the thoroughness of ISBD(A), increased in this country as planning for the North American participation in the *Eighteenth-Century Short Title Catalogue* (ESTC) commenced, and as the Library of Congress and other institutions around the country began to consider the question of rare book cataloging under AACR 2. The Operational Test of the ESTC (1978, Terry Belanger, Columbia University, School of Library Service, Project Director) addressed the problem, and the Independent Research Libraries Association's Ad Hoc Committee on Standards for Rare Book Cataloging in Machine-Readable Form (1978-79, Marcus McCorison, American Antiquarian Society, Chair) set the same issue high on its original agenda.

It was in this context that the Library of Congress began in June 1979 to prepare these rules for the descriptive cataloging of rare books under AACR 2, combining appropriate sections of Chapters 1 and 2 of those rules as well as the expanded provisions from the most recent — now the final — draft of ISBD(A). In preparing these rules, the Library was aided by the efforts of the Athenaeum Group (John Lancaster, Amherst College Library, Chair), an informal organization made up of administrators and cataloging staff from some dozen New England rare book libraries, which had first met in 1978 at the Boston Athenaeum as an informal adjunct to the IRLA Ad Hoc Committee, and which continued after the completion of the Ad Hoc Committee's work to study questions of rare book cataloging and computerized processing.

In addition, the Library has had valuable advice and comment from the staff of the North American Imprints Program at the American Antiquarian Society, which has assumed responsibility for supplying cataloging records to the ESTC for all 18th-century North American publications and which has already begun applying these rules in draft form.

A number of other libraries and individuals in the United States and Canada commented on earlier drafts of these rules, and the final text reflects many of these contributions.

---

[1] Finally published under the title *ISBD(A): International Standard Bibliographic Description for Older Monographic Publications (Antiquarian)*

These rules should be considered the Library of Congress' interpretation of AACR 2 Chapter 2 for its own cataloging of older printed materials. It is expected that the text may require revision over the course of time and comments on it from other institutions are welcomed.

* * *

These rules must be seen as supplementary to AACR 2. As stated in provision 0A, "Scope and Purpose," the general rules for the description of books, pamphlets, and printed sheets contained in AACR 2, Chapter 2 may be appropriate for some older or rare materials, depending on the policy of the cataloging institution. Even for publications cataloged under these rules, the text of AACR 2 proper must be applied for all aspects other than description (i.e., choice and form of access points, capitalization, etc.)

An important feature of these provisions for bibliographic description is that elements of data from a publication are generally transcribed as they appear, frequently without transposition or the other forms of intervention practiced by catalogers of ordinary books under AACR 2. This tendency requires that rare book catalogers be alert to the AACR 2 provisions for uniform titles and added entries as a means of making their records as accessible as those in which transposition, etc., occurs. For example, rule 1B2 says that subsidiary titles, etc., preceding the chief title should be transcribed in this position. In such cases, a uniform title should be assigned so that the record will file under the chief title; a title added entry should also be made for this chief title. Conversely, rule 1F for single sheet publications allows the transcription of a genuine chief title (an unusual occurrence with such material) with the omission of elements preceding this title on the sheet. A title added entry beginning with the words omitted is then essential so that anyone who does not recognize the chief title chosen by the cataloger may still have access to the record. These are merely two examples. The cataloger should be mindful of any such situations that require adding the proper access points to the bibliographic descriptions created under these provisions.

ACKNOWLEDGMENTS

Many individuals have contributed to the production of these rules. Lucia J. Rather, Director for Cataloging, Processing Services, Library of Congress, encouraged the effort from the start and gave generously of her time and knowledge to answer major policy questions raised by the committee she appointed to do the work. The committee was made up of present or former members of the Library of Congress staff, as follows: Stephen Paul Davis, Robert B. Ewald, Kay D. Guiles, J. William Matheson (also a member of the IFLA Working Group on ISBD(A)), Marion Schild, Roger J. Trienens, and Ben R. Tucker (Chair). Of equal importance to the Library of Congress committee was the fact that many individuals and institutions in the United States and Canada took time to comment on the draft of these rules, thereby sharing their expertise and knowledge with us.

I must mention specially the contributions made by the American Antiquarian Society and by the Athenaeum Group. In addition, I would like to acknowledge the cooperation and constructive criticism offered by Richard Christophers (British Library), who served as chair of the IFLA Working Group on ISBD(A). Finally, many thanks must go to Lisa Cockran for the long hours she spent at the Lexitron preparing this manuscript for publication.

Ben R. Tucker
Chief, Office for Descriptive Cataloging Policy

LIST OF WORKS CITED

Anglo-American Cataloguing Rules, Second Edition. 1988 Revision. Chicago: American Library Association, 1988.

Binding Terms: A Thesaurus for Use in Rare Book and Special Collections Cataloguing. Prepared by the Standards Committee of the Rare Books and Manuscripts Section. Chicago: Association of College and Research Libraries, 1988.

Bowers, Fredson T. Principles of Bibliographical Description. Princeton: Princeton University Press, 1949. [1986 reprint: Winchester, U.K.: St. Paul's Bibliographies]

British Museum. Catalogue of Books Printed in the XVth Century Now in the British Museum. London: British Museum, 1908- .

Cappelli, A. Cronologia e Calendario Perpetuo. Milano: Ulrico Hoepli, 1906. [3rd ed. Cronologia, Cronografia e Calendario Perpetuo. Milano: Ulrico Hoepli, 1969]

CONSER Editing Guide. Prepared by the staff of the Serial Record Division under the direction of the CONSER Operations Coordinator. Washington, D.C.: Serial Record Division, Library of Congress, 1986 (and updates).

Cowley, J.D. Bibliographical Description and Cataloguing. London: Grafton & Co., 1939. [1970 reprint: New York: Burt Franklin]

Descriptive Terms for Graphic Materials: Genre and Physical Characteristic Headings. Compiled and edited by Helena Zinkham and Elisabeth Betz Parker, Prints and Photographs Division, Library of Congress. Washington: Cataloging Distribution Service, Library of Congress, 1986.

Esdaile, Arundell. A Student's Manual of Bibliography. London: George Allen & Unwin & the Library Association, 1931. [5th rev. ed.: Esdaile's Manual of Bibliography. Metuchen, N.J.: Scarecrow Press, 1981]

Fingerprints = Empreintes = Impronte. Paris: Institut de Recherche et d'Histoire des Textes, 1984. Supplemented by: Nouvelles des empreintes = Fingerprint Newsletter (no. 1- 1981- Paris: Institut de Recherche et d'Histoire des Textes).

Gaskell, Philip. A New Introduction to Bibliography. Oxford: Clarendon Press, 1974 (c1972). "Reprinted with corrections."

Genre Terms: A Thesaurus for Use in Rare Book and Special Collections Cataloguing. Prepared by the Standards Committee of the Rare Books and Manuscripts Section. Chicago: Association of College and Research Libraries, 1983. And supplement: "Additions and Changes to Genre Terms: a Thesaurus." College & Research Libraries, v. 48, no. 9 (Oct. 1987), p. 558-560. [2nd ed. forthcoming, 1991]

Gesamtkatalog der Wiegendrucke. Herausgegeben von der Kommission für den Gesamtkatalog der Wiegendrucke. Leipzig: Verlag von Karl W. Hiersemann, 1925-

Hallam, Adele. Cataloging Rules for the Description of Looseleaf Publications. Washington, D.C.: Cataloging Distribution Service, Library of Congress, 1989. 2nd ed.

ISBD(A): International Standard Bibliographic Description for Older Monographic Publications (Antiquarian) [2nd ed. forthcoming, 1991]

McKerrow, R.B. An Introduction to Bibliography for Literary Students. Oxford: Oxford University Press, 1965 (c1927)

McKerrow, R.B. "Some notes on the letters i, j, u and v in sixteenth-century printing." The Library, 3rd series, no. 1 (1910)

Paper Terms: A Thesaurus for Use in Rare Book and Special Collections Cataloguing. Prepared by the Bibliographic Standards Committee of the Rare Books and Manuscripts Section. Chicago: Association of College and Research Libraries, 1990.

Printing and Publishing Evidence: Thesauri for Use in Rare Book and Special Collections Cataloguing. Prepared by the Standards Committee of the Rare Books and Manuscripts Section. Chicago: Association of College and Research Libraries, 1986.

Provenance Evidence: Thesaurus for Use in Rare Book and Special Collections Cataloguing. Prepared by the Standards Committee of the Rare Books and Manuscripts Section. Chicago: Association of College and Research Libraries, 1988.

"Relator Terms for Rare Book, Manuscript, and Special Collections Cataloguing." Prepared by the Standards Committee of the Rare Books and Manuscripts Section. 3rd ed. College & Research Libraries, v. 48, no. 9 (Oct. 1987), p. 553-557. [Supplemented by correction note on p. 645, v. 48, no. 10 (Nov. 1987)]

Tanselle, G. Thomas. "The bibliographical concepts of issue and state." In: Papers of the Bibliographical Society of America, v. 69 (1975), p. 17-66.

Type Evidence: A Thesaurus for Use in Rare Book and Special Collections Cataloguing. Prepared by the Bibliographic Standards Committee of the Rare Books and Manuscripts Section. Chicago: Association of College and Research Libraries, 1990.

USMARC Code List for Relators, Sources, Description Conventions. Prepared by Network Development and MARC Standards Office. Washington: Cataloging Distribution Service, Library of Congress, 1990.

USMARC Format for Bibliographic Data. Prepared by Network Development and MARC Standards Office. Washington: Cataloging Distribution Service, Library of Congress, 1988 (and updates)

VanWingen, Peter M. and Stephen Paul Davis. Standard Citation Forms for Published Bibliographies and Catalogs Used in Rare Book Cataloging. Washington: Library of Congress, 1982. And supplement: "Citation forms for bibliographies appearing in journals or as component parts of larger works." Prepared by the Standards Committee of the Rare Books and Manuscripts Section. College & Research Libraries News, v. 49, no. 8 (Sept. 1988), p. 525-526.

0. GENERAL RULES

Contents:

0A. Scope and purpose
0B. The basic description
0C. Chief source of information (title page)
0D. Prescribed sources of information
0E. Punctuation
0F. Language and script of the description
0G. Misprints, etc.
0H. Forms of diacritical marks and letters (including capitalization)
0J. Abbreviations
0K. Initials, etc.

0A. Scope and purpose

These rules are based on the 1988 Revision of the *Anglo-American Cataloguing Rules, Second Edition* (referred to hereafter as AACR 2) and on the revised *ISBD(A): International Standard Bibliographic Description for Older Monographic Publications (Antiquarian)*. They provide instructions for cataloging printed books, pamphlets, and single-sheet publications whose rarity, value, or interest make special description necessary or desirable. They are especially appropriate for such publications produced before the introduction of machine printing in the nineteenth century. They may be used in describing any book, however, particularly those produced by hand or by methods continuing the tradition of the hand-produced book.

Rare books often present situations not ordinarily encountered in the cataloging of the usual modern book (e.g., evidence of cancelled leaves) and may require details of description beyond what is required for the more ordinary book in order to identify significant characteristics (paper, type, etc.). These details are important for two reasons. They permit a ready identification of copies of the book (e.g., as editions, impressions, or issues), and they provide a more exact description of the book as an artifact.

These rules may either be applied categorically to books based on date or place of publication (e.g., all British and North American imprints published before 1801), or may be applied selectively, according to the administrative policy of the institution, which may choose to catalog some or all of its holdings at a more detailed level of description than that provided for in AACR 2.[2]

0B. The basic description

0B1. The description must always include the following elements, regardless of the completeness of the information available: title proper, date of publication, extent of item, size of item. Also include other elements of description as set out in the following rules whenever they are available.

---

[2]The Library of Congress applies these rules consistently to books published before 1801, rather than rules 2.12-2.18 of AACR 2, while generally applying AACR 2 proper to later publications.

0B2. In general, base the description on the copy in hand. If this copy is known to be imperfect, however, and the details of the description of a copy without the imperfection(s) can be determined with certainty, rely on these details, employing the conventions for bracketing (cf. 0E) as if the imperfection(s) did not exist. In such cases, the details should be verified by examining one or more additional copies, or by referring to a description in a reliable bibliography, preferably one based on an examination of several copies. Cite the source used for the description in a note (cf. 7C14).

If the copy being cataloged is imperfect and no reliable evidence of the necessary details is available, describe the copy as it is. Use the mark of omission enclosed in square brackets to show lacunae in the source of information if this helps to explain the incompleteness of the transcription. If missing or obscured letters or words can be reconstructed with some certainty, include these in the transcription, enclosing them in square brackets. Use the note area to justify such additions and to provide explanations, conjectural readings of the data, etc.

0C. Chief source of information (title page)

0C1. The chief source of information for a publication other than a broadside or a single sheet (see 1F) is the title page, or, if there is no title page, the source from within the publication that is used as a substitute for it. If information traditionally given on the title page is given on two facing pages or on pages on successive leaves, with or without repetition, treat these pages as the title page.

0C2. If the publication has more than one title page, choose one as the basis of the description according to the following guidelines, applying the first applicable criterion:

a)   If the title pages present the publication in different aspects (e.g., as an individual item and as part of a multipart item), prefer the one that corresponds to the aspect in which the publication is to be treated.

b)   If the publication is in more than one volume, each of which has a title page, use the title page in volume one (or the lowest numbered volume if volume one is not available).

c)   If the publication is in one volume and the chief difference between multiple title pages is imprint date, choose the one with the latest date.

d)   If the publication is in one volume and the chief difference between two title pages is that one is letterpress and the other is engraved, choose the letterpress title page.

e)   If the publication has the same title page in more than one language or script, choose the title page that is in the language or script of the main part of the publication.

f)   If two title pages face one another, choose the right-hand one (the one on the recto of its leaf).

g)   If two or more title pages follow one another, choose the first one.

Indicate in a note the title page chosen as the chief source of information if other than the usual title page, or, in a multivolume monograph, if it is other than the title page of volume one.

0C3. For publications issued without a title page (and for publications issued <u>with</u> a title page when the title page is missing and no reliable description of it is available), if a single title proper is available in a single source within the publication, use this source as the title page substitute. If the same title proper is available in more than one source within the publication, choose as the title page substitute the source that supplies the most additional title page information. If different titles, or differing forms of the same title, appear within the publication, select one as the title proper and use its source as the title page substitute. If for any reason this last mentioned provision does not settle the issue, choose as the title page substitute one of the following, according to the order given:

> a source within the preliminaries or the colophon
> a source elsewhere within the publication
> a source anywhere

Indicate in a note the source chosen as the title page substitute.

Hereafter in these rules, "title page" means "title page or title page substitute."

0D. Prescribed sources of information

The description is divided into areas and each area is divided into a number of elements as set out in the particular rules. For each area of the description (see the listing below), certain sources of information are specially indicated. Transcription of data from other sources is permissible, depending on the particular rules, but enclose these data from other sources within square brackets. The fact that data have been transcribed from one of the special sources, therefore, is indicated by the absence of square brackets. For the sole purpose of applying the convention of bracketing, these special sources are designated "prescribed sources." (For the preferred order of sources of information, see the particular rules for each area.)

Area	Prescribed Sources of Information
Title and statement of responsibility	Title page
Edition	Title page, other preliminaries, colophon
Publication, etc.	Title page, colophon, other preliminaries
Physical description	The whole publication
Series	Series title page, monograph title page, cover, rest of the publication
Note	Any source
Standard number and terms of availability	Any source

In all cases in which data for the first three areas are taken from elsewhere than the title page, make a note to indicate the source of the data.

The prescribed source of information for a single sheet publication in all the areas of the description, except the note area and the standard number and terms of availability area, is the entire sheet, both recto and verso. For the remaining two areas, information may be taken from any source without bracketing.

0E. Punctuation

Precede each area, other than the first, by a period-space-dash-space (. --) unless the area begins a new paragraph.

Precede or enclose each occurrence of an element of an area with standard punctuation as prescribed in these rules.

Precede each mark of prescribed punctuation by a space and follow it by a space, except for the comma, period, and opening and closing parentheses and square brackets. The comma, period, and closing parenthesis and square bracket are not preceded by a space; the opening parenthesis and square bracket are not followed by a space.

Precede the first element of each area, other than the first element of the first area or the first element of an area beginning a new paragraph, by a period-space-dash-space. If paragraphing is used, end paragraphs with normal punctuation (usually the period).

Generally follow conventions of modern punctuation in transcribing information according to these rules, except where ISBD marks of punctuation provide the punctuation. Otherwise, common sense may be used in transcribing or omitting punctuation found in the source. *Optionally*, record all of the punctuation that is found in the source of information. When this option is chosen, always give the prescribed punctuation as well, even if this results in double punctuation.

On title page:
Les pommes de terre, considérées relativement à la santé & à l'économie: ouvrage dans lequel on traite aussi du froment & du riz; par M. Parmentier

Transcription:
Les pommes de terre, considérées relativement à la santé & à l'économie : ouvrage dans lequel on traite aussi du froment & du riz / par M. Parmentier

Optional transcription:
Les pommes de terre, considérées relativement à la santé & à l'économie: : ouvrage dans lequel on traite aussi du froment & du riz; / par M. Parmentier

Whenever the mark of omission is used, generally give it with a space on either side (...). When indicating lacunae in the source, enclose the mark of omission in square brackets ([...]).

When an entire element or area is not present in the source, hence not transcribed, omit the corresponding prescribed punctuation from the transcription and do not use the mark of omission.

When omitting information from the source that is not considered part of any area (pious invocations, etc.; cf. 1A2) and not grammatically connected, do not use the mark of omission.

Indicate an interpolation (i.e., data taken from outside the prescribed source(s) of information) by enclosing it in square brackets. Indicate a conjectural interpolation by adding a question mark after the data, within the square brackets.

When adjacent elements within one area are to be enclosed in square brackets, generally enclose them in one set of square brackets.

[Leipzig : W. Stürmer], 1572

When the brackets are due to interpolations such as corrections (cf. 0J2), however, use separate pairs of brackets.

Christinia [Oslo] : [J. Hanson], 1781

When adjacent elements are in different areas, enclose each element in a set of square brackets.

[2nd ed.]. -- [London] : J. Bascom, printer, 1710

When a virgule (/) is used as a comma, either transcribe it as a comma or omit it. If desired, make a note to indicate the presence of the virgule in the source.

Do not transcribe the punctuation marks ... or [ ] when present in the source; replace them by -- and ( ) respectively.

0F. Language and script of the description

In the following areas, give information transcribed from the publication itself in the language and script (wherever practicable) in which it appears there:

> Title and statement of responsibility
> Edition
> Publication, etc.
> Series

Replace symbols or other matter that cannot be reproduced by the typographical facilities available[3] with a cataloger's description in square brackets. Make an explanatory note if necessary.

In general, give interpolations into these areas in the language and script of the other data in the area, except for prescribed interpolations and other cases specified in these rules, e.g., 1G9, 4B4, 4C6.

If the other data of the context are romanized, give interpolations according to the same romanization.

Give any other data (other than titles and quotations in notes) in English.

0G. Misprints, etc.

In an area where transcription from the publication is required, transcribe a misprint as it appears in the publication. Follow such an inaccuracy either by "[sic]" or by the abbreviation "i.e." and the correction within square brackets. Supply missing letters in square brackets.

> An hnmble [sic] address
> The notted [i.e. noted] history of Mother Grim
> One day's d[u]ty

Do not correct words spelled according to older or non-standard orthographic conventions, e.g., "françoise" for "française," or "antient" for "ancient."

When the printer has left blank space for an initial letter, give the letter without square brackets, regardless of whether a guide letter is present or the letter has been filled in by hand. Make a note to show the copy's actual state in this respect.

> Historiarum libri XXXV
> *Note:* Space for initial letter of first word of title left blank by printer
> *Note:* LC copy: Initial letter supplied in red and green ink

---

[3]At the Library of Congress, the typographical facilities referred to here and in succeeding rules include those characters available in the MARC character set.

0H. Forms of diacritical marks and letters (including capitalization)

In general do not add accents and other diacritical marks that are not present in the source.

In general transcribe letters as they appear. Convert earlier forms of letters and diacritical marks, however, to their modern form (cf. Appendix B). In most languages, including Latin, transcribe a ligature by giving its component letters separately. Do not, however, separate the component letters of æ in Anglo-Saxon; œ in French; or æ and œ in ancient or modern Scandinavian languages. (For the transcription of i/j and u/v, see below.) When there is any doubt as to the correct conversion of elements to modern form, transcribe them from the source as exactly as possible.

Convert to uppercase or lowercase according to the rules for capitalization in AACR 2, appendix A. (For roman numerals, see the specific rules and AACR 2, appendix C.) When the rules for capitalization require converting i/j or u/v to uppercase or lowercase, adhere to the pattern of uppercase/lowercase employed by the particular printer.[4] Only when a pattern cannot be determined should the following table for conversion be applied, for it represents a solution of last resort.

Transcribe into lowercase:

> I or J as i
> II as ii
> IJ as ij
> U or V as u (but U or V in initial position as v)
> VV as uu (or vv in initial position)

Transcribe into uppercase:

> i as I
> j as J
> u or v as V
> uu or vv as VV (i.e., two capital V's)

<u>Examples</u>

Title page:
ADVERTISSEMENT SVR LES IVGEMENS D'ASTROLOGIE
Transcription:
Aduertissement sur les iugemens d'astrologie
(In lowercase printer uses "i" and "u" forms)

Title page:
AN ABSTRACT OF THE LAVVES OF NEVV ENGLAND, As they are novv established
Transcription:
An abstract of the lavves of Nevv England, as they are novv established
(In lowercase printer uses double-v)

---

[4]For information on early printing as it pertains to the transcription of i/j and u/v, see Appendix B.

> *Title page:*
> HVGONIS GROTII DE IVRE BELLI AC PACIS LIBRI TRES. In quibus jus naturae &
> gentium : item juris publici praecipua explicantur
> *Transcription:*
> Hugonis Grotii De jure belli ac pacis libri tres
> *(Printer uses "j" form in initial position and "u" form in medial position)*

Do not convert to lowercase a final capital I when the preceding letters of the word are printed either in lowercase or in smaller capitals.

> *Title page:*
> M. Accl Plauti quae supersunt Comoediae
> *Transcription:*
> M. Accl Plauti quae supersunt Comoediae

Treat gothic capitals in the forms J and U as I and V. (In "modern" gothic where lowercase i and j are distinguished, transcribe the gothic capitals according to the lowercase usage.)

Capital letters occurring apparently at random or in a particular sequence on a title page or in a colophon may represent a chronogram. Where there is good reason to assume that a chronogram is being used, do not convert letters considered part of the chronogram from uppercase to lowercase, or from lowercase to uppercase. See also 4D2.

0J. Abbreviations

0J1. In an area where transcription from the publication is required, do not abbreviate any word except as permitted by 2B1.

0J2. When special marks of contraction have been used by the printer in continuance of the manuscript tradition, expand affected words to their full form and enclose supplied letters in square brackets. When an abbreviation standing for an entire word appears in the source, record instead the word itself, and enclose it in square brackets. If the Tironian sign (⁊) cannot be reproduced, treat it as an abbreviation and substitute "[et]" for it. Transcribe an ampersand as an ampersand. Enclose each expansion or supplied word in its own set of square brackets, e.g., "... amico[rum] [et] ..."

> Esopus co[n]structus moralizat[us] [et] hystoriatus ad vtilitate[m] discipulo[rum]

When the meaning of an abbreviation or contraction is conjectural, use the question mark after the supplied letters or word within the same set of brackets, e.g., " ... amico[rum?] [et] ..." When the meaning of an abbreviation or contraction cannot be determined, substitute a question mark within brackets for each element in question, e.g., " ... amico[?] [?] ..."

0K. Initials, etc.

Record initials, initialisms, and acronyms without internal spaces, regardless of how they are presented in the source of information. Apply this provision also whether or not these elements are presented with periods.

> Pel battesimo di S.A.R. Ludovico ...
> KL Ianuarius habet dies xxxi
> Monasterij B.M.V. Campililioru[m]
> J.J. Rousseau

Treat an abbreviation consisting of more than a single letter as if it were a distinct word, separating it with a space from preceding and succeeding words or initials.

> Ph. D.
> Ad bibliothecam PP. Franciscan. in Anger
> Mr. J.P. Morgan

If two or more distinct initialisms (or sets of initials), acronyms, or abbreviations appear in juxtaposition, separate each from the other with a space.

> M. J.P. Rabaut
> *(The first initial stands for Monsieur)*

1. TITLE AND STATEMENT OF RESPONSIBILITY AREA

Contents:

1A. Preliminary rule
1B. Title proper
1C. Parallel titles
1D. Other title information
1E. Publications without a collective title
1F. Single sheet publications
1G. Statements of responsibility

1A. Preliminary rule

1A1. Punctuation

For instructions on the use of spaces before and after prescribed punctuation, see 0E.

Precede the title of a supplement or section (see 1B6) by a period.

Precede each parallel title by an equals sign.

Precede each unit of other title information by a colon.

Precede the first statement of responsibility by a diagonal slash.

Precede each subsequent statement of responsibility by a semicolon.

For the punctuation of this area when a publication has no collective title, see 1E.

1A2. Sources of information.

Take information recorded in this area from the title page. Enclose information recorded from any other source in square brackets, and indicate its source in a note. For special provisions relating to single-sheet publications, see 1F.

Record the data in the prescribed order, subject to the limitations stated in these rules. Generally do not use the mark of omission to indicate transposition.

Omit, without using the mark of omission, information found on the title page that constitutes neither title information nor a statement of responsibility. Such information may include pious invocations, devices, announcements, epigrams, dedications, mottoes, statements of patronage, prices, etc. (cf. 0E). Use the note area to record or describe this kind of information if it is considered important. If such information is an inseparable part (see 1B1) of one of the elements of the title and statement of responsibility area, however, transcribe it as such. If such information constitutes the only title-like information present in the source, it may be used as a supplied title according to the provisions of 1B5.

When the volume is part of a multivolume monograph, and the title page gives a statement of the volume or part number within the larger work, omit this statement without using the mark of omission, unless it is an inseparable part (cf. 1B1, 1B4) of the information being transcribed. Do transcribe statements such as "in two volumes," however (cf. 1D3).

1B. Title proper[5]

1B1. The title proper is the first element of the description. Parallel titles, other titles, and other title information preceding the chief title on the title page are considered part of the title proper. If the chief title is preceded or followed in the source by other elements of information, transpose these elements to their appropriate areas in the record (or give them in a note) unless case endings would be affected, the grammatical construction of the data would be disturbed, or the element is otherwise inseparably linked to the title proper. In the latter cases, transcribe the data as part of the title proper.

> The post-humous works of Robert Hooke
> Monsieur Bossu's treatise of the epicke poem
> Thomas Masterson his first booke of arithmeticke ...
> M. Tullii Ciceronis De officiis libri tres
>
> Le premier volume de messire Jehan Froissart lequel traicte des choses dignes de mémoire aduenues tant en ce pays de France ...
>
> Bell's edition of Shakspere

Make a note to indicate the original position on the title page of transposed elements.

Indicate in a note the source of the title proper if it is a title page substitute, e.g., the caption title.

1B2. Transcribe the title proper according to general rules 0B-0K.

1B3. The title proper can take a variety of forms, some of which are exemplified below:

Titles proper inclusive of other titles or other title information appearing before the title proper on the title page:

> Seculum Davidicum redivivum, The divine right of the revolution scripturally and rationally evinced and applied
> *(By virtue of its typographical prominence, the English title is clearly the chief title)*
>
> Prize dissertation, which was honored with the Magellanic Gold Medal, by the American Philosophical Society, January, 1793. Cadmus: or, A treatise on the elements of written language
> *(Cadmus ... is clearly more prominent than Prize dissertation ...)*
>
> Hereafter foloweth a litel boke called Colyn Cloute

---

[5]See the definitions of "chief title" and "title proper" in the Glossary.

Titles proper inclusive of alternative titles:

> Christianographie, or, The description of the multitude and sundry sorts of Christians in
> the vvorld not subject to the Pope

Titles proper consisting solely of the name of a responsible person or body:

> Salustius
> Diss bŭch heÿusset Lucidarius

Titles proper inclusive of a caption (see 1F for caption titles on single-sheet publications):

> *First page:*
> To the Honourable Commissioners appointed by Act of Parliament for enquiring into the
> Losses and Services of the American Loyalists. The memorial of Silvester Gardiner
> humbly sheweth, ...
>
> *Transcription:*
> To the honourable commisioners appointed by act of Parliament for enquiring into the
> losses and services of the American loyalists. The memorial of Silvester Gardiner ...

1B4. If a publication is in more than one volume and the title proper of each volume includes a designation such as numbering that is specific to that volume, add in square brackets after the first designation a hyphen and the final designation, omitting intermediate designations.

> Quinti Horatii Flacci Epistolarum liber primus[-secundus]

If it is not practicable to do this, transcribe the title proper of the first volume without this addition and make a note about the later designation(s).

1B5. If no title can be found in any source, use as the title proper the opening words of the text if these provide a relatively distinctive title. If the opening words of the text are not suitable, or if the beginning of the text is lacking, devise a brief descriptive title, preferably in English, and use this devised title, enclosed in square brackets, as the title proper. Indicate in a note whether the title proper is taken from the opening words of the text or has been devised by the cataloger.

> I am a jolly huntsman, my voice is shrill and clear
> *(Title is not bracketed because the first page of text is here the title page substitute)*
> *Note:* Title from opening two lines of poem
>
> [Observations on a bill relative to the militia]
> *(Opening words "Herewith and the desire of being serviceable in the smallest degree to
> my country ..." not suitable as title)*
> *Note:* Title devised from content
>
> [A Sermon on Christian baptism]
> *Note:* Title devised from content of sermon

1B6. If the title proper for a work that is supplementary to, or a section of, another work appears in two or more parts not grammatically linked, transcribe the title of the main work first, followed by the title(s) of the supplement(s) or section(s) in order of their dependence. Separate the parts of the title proper by periods. When the arrangement indicated requires transposition, make a note to indicate the actual reading of the titles.

> Faust. Part one
> *Note:* Title page reads: Part one. Faust

1B7. In general, do not abridge the title proper. Exceptionally, when the title proper is very lengthy and can be abridged without loss of essential information, omit less important words or phrases, indicating the abridgement with the mark of omission. Never abridge the title proper before the sixth word except in certain cases involving an alternative title: When the title proper is very lengthy and contains an alternative title, the entire alternative title may be omitted without regard for the number of words remaining in the title proper.

Extend the transcription of the title proper through to the end of the chief title of the publication. Apply this provision even if other elements (cf. 1B1, 1B3) precede the chief title. If the end of the chief title cannot be determined, break off the transcription at the first tolerable place, but in no event before the sixth word.

> Jo. Danielis Schoepflini consil. reg. ac Franciae historiogr. Vindiciae typographicae

> M. Georg Wolfgang Panzers, Schaffers an der Hauptpfarrkirche bey St. Sebald in Nürnberg, und des Pegnerischen Blumenordens daselbst Praeses, Aelteste Buchdruckergeschichte Nürnbergs

> An act or law passed by the General Court or Assembly of His Majesty's English Colony of Connecticut ... on the seventh day of February ... 1759

1C. Parallel titles

Transcribe parallel titles in the order indicated by their sequence on, or by the layout of, the title page.

Transcribe an original title in a language different from that of the title proper appearing on the title page as a parallel title if it is not grammatically linked to another part of the description. Transcribe an original title in the same language as the title proper as other title information (see 1D).

> Fables = Fabulae
> The adventures of Red Riding Hood : Little Red Riding Hood

If an original title appears elsewhere than on the title page, give it in a note.

1D. Other title information

1D1. Transcribe other title information appearing on the title page in the order indicated by the sequence on, or layout of, the title page. Transcribe other title information not appearing on the title page in a note whenever it is considered important.

1D2. Ordinarily transcribe other titles or phrases following the title proper as other title information even if they are linked to the title proper by a preposition, conjunction, prepositional phrase, etc.

> The English Parliament represented in a vision : with an after-thought upon the speech delivered to His Most Christian Majesty by the deputies of the states of Britany on the 29th day of February last ... : to which is added at large the memorable representation of the House of Commons to the Queen in the year 1711/12 ...

When statements of this kind appear following the statement of responsibility, punctuate them as subsequent statements of responsibility (cf. 1G14).

If these other titles or phrases constitute a formal statement of the contents of the work, however, give them in the note area (cf. 7C16) unless they are an inseparable part of the title proper or of other title information. When these formal statements are omitted from the title and statement of responsibility area, use the mark of omission.

> The spinning wheel's garland : containing several excellent new songs ...
>
> Note: Contents: (from t.p.) I. The good housewife's coat of arms -- II. The spinning wheels glory -- III. The taylor disappointed of his bride -- IV. The changeable world

Distinguish the above situations from those in which the titles of the other works are given equal prominence with the first-named work (cf. 1E1).

1D3. Generally treat statements such as "in two volumes" as other title information (cf. also 2B8).

1D4. When other title information is very lengthy and can be abridged without loss of essential information, omit less important words or phrases, using the mark of omission. If desired, give in a note other title information not transcribed (including the other titles or phrases referred to in 1D2).

1D5. If the other title information includes a statement of responsibility or an element belonging to another area, and the element is an inseparable part of the other title information according to one or more of the conditions enumerated in 1B1, transcribe it as such.

> Constitutiones legitime seu legative regionis Anglicane : cu[m] subtilissima interpretatione Johannis de Athon
> *(Statement of responsibility transcribed as part of other title information because of genitive case ending)*

1D6. Transcribe parallel other title information in the order in which it appears on the title page.

1E. Publications without a collective title

1E1. When a publication has no collective title and the title page bears the titles of two or more individual works, other than supplementary matter, that are contained in the publication, transcribe the titles of the individual works in the order in which they appear on the title page. Separate the titles of the parts by a space-semicolon-space if the parts are all by the same person(s) or body (bodies), even though the titles are linked by a connecting word or phrase.

> Les Akanças : prologue mélo-dramatique, en un acte et en prose ; suivi Des Espagnols
> dans la Floride : pantomime en trois actes et à spectacle

If the individual works are by different persons or bodies, or the authorship is in doubt, precede the title of each part other than the first by a period and one space, unless a linking word or phrase is already present. Precede each statement of responsibility by a space-slash-space.

> The serving-man become a queen. Jockey of the green. The lass of Richmond Hill.

1E2. When a publication has no collective title, and works additional to those named on the title page appear in the publication, whether or not on pages laid out as title pages, either transcribe the titles of such works according to the provisions of 1E1 (in square brackets), or give them in the note area (cf. 7C16).

> Prima[-decima] egloga della Bucolica di Virgilio / p[er] B. Pulci dilatino in uulgare
> traducta. [Elegia di Bernardo Pulci a Lorenzo de Medeci per lamorte di Cosimo ;
> Bernardus Pulcius Florentinus de obitu Diue Simonette. Francisci de Arsochis Senensis
> carmen bucolicum ... Buccolica di Hieronymo Beniuiene fiorentino. Bucolica di Iacopo
> Fiorino]
>
> *Note:* No collective title; individual titles taken from leaves a6, e6, f2, g1, h7, and m4 verso

Alternatively, if the preceding method does not provide satisfactory results, devise a collective title for the whole publication (Cf. 1B5).

> [A collection of acts of Parliament enacted in 1732]

1F. Single sheet publications

1F1. For single sheet publications, take information for the title and statement of responsibility area from the recto and/or the verso of the sheet without bracketing.

1F2. Generally transcribe the data presented beginning with the first line of printing. If the printing is arranged in columns with no data preceding the body of the text, begin the transcription with the top line of the extreme left column (extreme right column in the case of languages that are read right-left). Generally retain in the transcription dates, addresses, and other data necessary for identification. Use judgment, but in case of doubt, start the transcription with the first element. If the first element on the sheet is not integrated with the succeeding material and is an element such as one of the following, however, begin the transcription after it (without using the mark of omission):

> caption to an illustration
> copyright statement
> device
> edition statement
> imprint statement
> motto
> official numbering
> page number
> part of an illustration or ornament
> price
> tabular material

If the first element has been omitted, generally indicate the nature and position of the omitted material in a note.

1F3. If there is a word or phrase obviously intended as the chief title of the publication that is not the first line of printing, transcribe it as the entire title proper, omitting elements appearing before it on the page without the mark of omission. (In general, this instruction should be applied only when such a title is not integrated grammatically with the rest of the data, is set off typographically, and has as its sole function the naming of the piece as a whole.) When such a title is selected, also give in a note at least the first five words of the first line of printing as described above. In case of doubt as to the selection of the chief title, start the transcription with the first line as described above.

1F4. If a caption title is present, normally transcribe this title in full. If there is no caption title, transcribe the data at least until a relatively distinctive word or phrase is included. If the distinctive word or phrase is not near the beginning of the transcription, less important words or phrases ahead of it may be omitted, using the mark of omission. Do not, however, abridge the transcription before the sixth word. If the data are very lengthy, end the transcription at the first grammatically acceptable place after the caption title or the distinctive word or phrase; the omitted material may be summarized in a note.

1F5. Information transcribed from single sheet publications will generally not lend itself to the application of the punctuation prescribed in 1A1 for the title and statement of responsibility area. If, however, the information can be separated clearly and unmistakably into title proper, other title information, or statement of responsibility without any transposition, supply the prescribed punctuation.

1F6. If there are two or more works printed on a single sheet having a collective title, transcribe only the collective title as the title proper. Make a formal or informal contents note for the works.

1F7. If there are two or more works printed on a single sheet that does not have a collective title, transcribe as the title statement the first title or opening words of the text. Make a formal or informal contents note and include in it the titles of the additional works. If the sheet is printed on both sides and it is impossible to determine which side should be read first, make a separate cataloging record for each side of the sheet, and include a formal "With, on verso:" note in each record (cf. 7C19).

1F8. If there are two or more works printed on a single sheet and each has its own imprint or there is other conclusive evidence that they were intended to be separately issued, make a separate catalog record for each work that was intended to be issued separately. Include a formal "With:" note in each record (see 7C19) indicating that the works were printed on a single sheet and that they were "intended to be separated." If there are two or more works printed on a single sheet giving the appearance that they were possibly intended to be separated, but there is no conclusive evidence that this is the case, follow the provisions of 1F7, and include a note indicating that they were "possibly intended to be separated."

1G. Statements of responsibility

1G1. Transcribe statements of responsibility appearing in the preliminaries (title page recto and verso, cover, and any page preceding the title page) or in the colophon, in the form in which they appear. If a statement of responsibility is not taken from the title page, enclose it in square brackets and indicate its source in a note.

> The history of the long captivity and adventures of Thomas Pellow, in South-Barbary ... / written by himself
>
> De indiciis et praecognitionibus : opus apprime utile medicis / Dauide Edguardo Anglo authore
>
> I dieci libri di architettura / di Leon Battista Alberti
> Thoughts on education / by the late Bishop Burnet
>
> The whole body of antient and modern architecture : comprehending what has been said of it by these ten principal authors ... / [by Roland Freart, sr. de Chambray]
> *Note:* Author statement from added engraved t.p.

1G2. If a statement of responsibility appears in a source other than the title page, other preliminaries, or the colophon, or if it is taken from outside the publication, give it in the note area.

> Note: Pref. signed: Thomas Hopkins
> *(Hopkins is not recorded in the statement of responsibility area even though he is known to be the author)*
>
> Note: "By an engineer"--Introd.

1G3. If a statement of responsibility precedes the title proper in the source, transpose it to its required position unless it is an inseparable part of the title proper according to one or more of the conditions enumerated in 1B1. When transposing the statement of responsibility, do not use the mark of omission. Make a note indicating this transposition.

> Hanc dissertationem medicam de hydrope tympanite ... submittit ad diem Martii
> M.Dc.LXXII ... David Richter, Zittâ-Lusatus, autor / praeside ... Dn. Johanne Arnoldo
> Friderici.
>
> *Note:* Blank space left by printer following "diem" on title page
>
> *Note:* "Praeside" statement precedes title on title page

1G4. Transcribe a single statement of responsibility as such whether the two or more persons or corporate bodies named in it perform the same function or different functions.

> Puzzled people : a study in popular attitudes to religion, ethics, progress, and politics in
> a London borough / prepared for the Ethical Union by Mass-Observation
>
> A new method of discovering the longitude both at sea and land ... / by William Whiston
> and Humphry Ditton
>
> A treatise of health and long life, with the sure means of attaining it : in two books / the
> first by Leonard Lessius, the second by Lewis Cornaro ...

When a respondent and praeses are given for an academic disputation, treat both names and the words indicative of their function as part of a single statement of responsibility (unless grammatically linked to the title proper or to other title information).

> / pro disputatione publica proponebatur praeside Jacobo Fabricio, respondente Johanne
> Reembbelt
>
> *but*   De peripneumonia disputationem ... sub praesidio ... Dn. Jacobi Fabricii ... publice
> examinandam proponit Johannes Hellinger

1G5. When a single statement of responsibility names more than one person or corporate body performing the same function or with the same degree of responsibility, generally transcribe all the names mentioned. If the number of responsible persons or bodies named in a single statement is very great, all after the third may be omitted. Indicate the omission by the mark of omission and add "et al." in square brackets.

1G6. If there are two or more statements of responsibility, give them in the order indicated by their sequence on, or by the layout of, the title page. If the sequence and layout are ambiguous or insufficient to determine the order, give the statements in the order that makes the most sense. If statements of responsibility appear in sources other than the title page, also transcribe them in the order that makes the most sense.

> El Fuero real de España / diligentemente hecho por el noble Rey don Alonso noveno ;
> glossado por Alonso Díaz de Montalvo ...

1G7. Include titles and abbreviations of titles of nobility, address, honor, and distinction that appear with names in statements of responsibility.

> / by M. d'Alembert ...
> / by Horatio Walpole, Earl of Orford ...

1G8. Generally omit from the statement of responsibility such qualifications as initials indicating membership in societies, academic degrees, statements of positions held unless:

	a)	the elements are necessary grammatically
or	b)	the elements are necessary for identifying the person or are useful in establishing a context for the person's activity (initials of religious orders, phrases or adjectives denoting place names, etc.)
or	c)	the statement of responsibility represents the author only by a pseudonym, a descriptive phrase, or nonalphabetic symbols.

Use the mark of omission to indicate any such elements omitted.

1G9. If desired, add a word or short phrase in English, within square brackets, to the statement of responsibility when the relationship between the title of the work and the person(s) or body (bodies) named in the statement is not clear.

> Morte Arthure / [edited by] John Finlayson

Give expansions, explanations, and corrections of statements of responsibility in the note area when needed for clarity (cf. 7C6).

1G10. If there are parallel titles but a statement of responsibility in only one language or script, transcribe the statement of responsibility after all the parallel titles or other title information.

> Jeux de cartes pour enfants = Children's playing cards / par Giovanni Belgrado et
> Bruno Munari

If there are parallel titles and a statement or statements of responsibility in more than one language or script, transcribe each statement after the title proper, parallel title, or other title information to which it relates. When any of these titles lacks a matching statement of responsibility, record the elements in the order indicated by the sequence on, or by the layout of, the title page.

> Anatomia uteri humani gravidi tabulis illustrata / auctore Gulielmo Hunter ... = The
> anatomy of the human gravid uterus exhibited in figures / by William Hunter

1G11. Treat a noun or noun phrase occurring in conjunction with a statement of responsibility as other title information if it is indicative of the nature of the work.

> Comus : a mask / by John Milton

If the noun or noun phrase is indicative of the role of the person(s) or body (bodies) named in the statement of responsibility rather than of the nature of the work, treat it as part of the statement of responsibility.

> Paradise lost : a poem in twelve books / the author John Milton
> A cushion of downe / text by Gilbert Frye ; drawings by Charles Cox

In case of doubt, treat the noun or noun phrase as part of the statement of responsibility.

1G12. Transcribe a statement of responsibility as such even if no person or body is explicitly named in that statement. (Such statements will generally contain words like "translated," "edited," "compiled," etc.)

> The folouuing of Christ / translated out of Latin into English

1G13. If the statement of responsibility includes an element belonging to another area, and the element is an inseparable part of the statement of responsibility according to one or more of the conditions enumerated in 1B1, transcribe it as part of the statement of responsibility.

> L'hymne au soleil / traduit en vers latins, sur la troisième édition du texte françois, par
> M. l'abbé Métivier

1G14. Transcribe phrases about notes, appendices, and such accompanying matter in the order indicated by the sequence on the title page. Accordingly, when such statements appear before the statement of responsibility, punctuate them as other title information (cf. 1D2).

> Chemische Erfahrungen bey meinem und andern Fabriken in Deutschland : nebst einem Anhang besonderer chemischer Geheimnisse / von J.A. Weber

> Clarion call : with Franklin Phelps' criticisms / by Lunceford Yates

When such phrases are transcribed after the statement of responsibility, punctuate them as subsequent statements of responsibility, whether or not they name a person or body.

> High life below stairs : a farce / by James Townley ; with a variety of German notes explanatory of the idioms ... alluded to by John Christian Huttner

> Some remarks on the Barrier Treaty, between Her Majesty and the States-General / by the author of The conduct of the allies ; to which are added the said Barrier-Treaty ; with the two separate articles ...

> Monsieur Bossu's treatise of the epick poem ... / done into English from the French, with a new original preface upon the same subject, by W.J. ; to which are added, An essay upon Satyr, by Monsieur d'Acier ; and A treatise upon pastorals, by Monsieur Fontanelle

If the phrases are lengthy, omit them using the mark of omission. If important, phrases omitted may be given in a note. If the phrases are actually titles of other works given equal prominence with the title of the first work, however, see 1E.

2. EDITION AREA

Contents:

2A. Preliminary rule

2A1. Punctuation

For instructions on the use of spaces before and after prescribed punctuation, see 0E.

Precede the edition area by a period-space-dash-space.

Precede a statement relating to a named revision of an edition by a comma.

Precede the first statement of responsibility following an edition statement by a diagonal slash.

Precede each subsequent statement of responsibility by a semicolon.

2A2. Sources of information

The prescribed sources of information for the edition area are the title page, other preliminaries, and colophon, in that order of preference. If an edition statement is not present in any of these sources, take it from any source within the publication and enclose it within square brackets. If the edition statement, or any part of the edition area, is taken from elsewhere than the title page, indicate its source in the note area.

2B. Edition statement

2B1. Transcribe the statement relating to an edition of a publication in the terms in which it appears. Give the exact wording if the edition statement is taken from the title page. If it is taken from any other source, standard abbreviations and arabic numerals may be given in place of words. Include explanatory words or phrases appearing with the edition statement.

2B2. Transcribe as an edition statement a statement relating to issues or impressions, even if the publication contains no changes from the previous edition.

2B3. The edition statement normally includes either the word "edition" (or its equivalent in other languages), or a related term such as "revision" or "issue." Treat a phrase such as "newly printed" as an edition statement unless it is part of a statement being transcribed in the publication area.

> The second edition
>
> [2nd ed.]
> *Note:* Edition statement from verso of title page
>
> Cinquiesme édition, reueuë, corrigée, & augmentée
>
> Newly imprinted and very necessary vnto all youthe
> *(But use as part of imprint: Philadelphia printed, London reprinted)*
>
> Nunc primum in lucem aedita
> Editio secunda auctior et correctior

2B4. When the edition statement consists entirely or chiefly of characters that are neither numeric nor alphabetic, transcribe the characters as they appear if the necessary typographical facilities are available. For those characters that cannot be reproduced, substitute the names or descriptions of the characters in English in square brackets.

> &&& ed.
> [alpha chi] ed.

When the edition statement consists of one or more letters or numbers without accompanying words, add an appropriate word or abbreviation in the language of the title proper, in square brackets.

> 3e [éd.]
> [State] B
> 2[nd print.]

2B5. When the publication does not contain an edition statement, but is known to contain significant changes from other editions, or an edition statement for it is provided by a reference source, give this information in a note.

> *Note:* 'Sixth ed.'--Tchemerzine, v. 6, p. 117-131

2B6. When an edition statement is an inseparable part of another area according to one or more of the conditions enumerated in 1B1, and has been transcribed as such, do not repeat it as an edition statement.

> Old New York, or, Reminiscences of the past sixty years : being an enlarged and
> revised edition of the anniversary discourse delivered before the New York Historical
> Society ...
>
> Chirurgia / nunc iterum non mediocri studio atque diligentia a pluribus mendis purgata

2B7. Transpose separable edition statements into the edition area from other parts of the title page. If desired, make a note indicating this transposition.

2B8. When information pertaining to other elements of the description (e.g., an original title or other information concerning the original work) is an inseparable part of an edition statement according to one or more of the conditions enumerated in 1B1, transcribe it as part of the edition statement. When statements such as "in two volumes" appear with an edition statement, transcribe them as they appear (cf. also 1D3).

2B9. When the publication bears edition statements in more than one language or script, transcribe the statement that is in the language or script of the title proper. If this criterion does not apply, transcribe the statement that appears first. Apply the same instructions to any associated statements of responsibility in more than one language or script. Give parallel statements, together with any associated statements of responsibility, in a note if desired.

2C. Statements of responsibility relating to the edition

2C1. Transcribe a statement of responsibility relating to one or more editions, but not to all editions, of a given work following the edition statement if there is one. Such statements may include the reviser or illustrator of a new edition, or a corporate body responsible for a new edition. Follow the instructions in 1G for the transcription and punctuation of such statements of responsibility.

> The second edition / with notes of various authors by Thomas Newton

Do not, however, apply this provision to such statements that do not name a person or corporate body.

> The second edition revised and corrected
> *Not:*   The second edition / revised and corrected

In determining the extent of the edition statement and the beginning of the statement of responsibility relating to the edition, it may be necessary to take into account the layout, punctuation, and typography of the title page as well as the sense of the text. Such words as "Revised and enlarged," when appearing with the name of a person or body, might be transcribed either as part of the edition statement or as part of the statement of responsibility relating to the edition, depending on their presentation on the title page.

2C2. When a statement of responsibility appears after the edition statement, transpose it to the title and statement of responsibility area in all cases except when it clearly applies only to the edition being cataloged. Make a note to indicate this transposition.

> An inquiry into the original state and formation of the earth : deduced from facts about the laws of nature / by John Whitehurst. -- The second edition, considerably enlarged, and illustrated with plates
> *(Statement of responsibility applies to all editions)*
> *Note:* The statement "by John Whitehurst" appears on the title page after the edition statement

2C3. If there are phrases about notes, appendices, and such supplementary matter and they apply to the edition in hand but not necessarily to all editions of the work, transcribe them as statements of responsibility relating to the edition only in the case when the phrase names or otherwise identifies a person or corporate body and appears in the same source as the edition statement.

> The fourth edition / with a new epilogue by the author
> Editio altera, ab innumeris erroribus emendata / huic editioni accessere Jacobi Bongarsii Excerptiones chronologicae ad Justini historias accommodatae

When the phrase does not name a person or corporate body, transcribe it as part of the edition statement proper or as part of the first statement of responsibility relating to the edition, as appropriate. Do not introduce the semicolon (as in 1G14) to separate such phrases from preceding statements of responsibility.

> The fourth edition, with notes

> A new edition / by Grace Webster, to which is added a life of the author

If such phrases have been transposed from a position preceding the edition statement, make a note if desired to indicate this transposition.

2D. Statement relating to a named revision of an edition

2D1. When a publication is a revision of a particular edition and has a statement to this effect, transcribe this statement following the edition statement and its statements of responsibility, if any.

> The third edition, Reprinted with a new preface

2D2. Transcribe a statement relating to the revision of an edition according to the applicable provisions of 2B.

24

2D3. Transcribe also statements of unchanged impressions of an edition (cf. 2B2).

> The second edition, The fifth impression

2E. Statements of responsibility relating to a named revision of an edition

2E1. Transcribe a statement of responsibility relating to a named revision of an edition following the statement relating to the revision.

2E2. Transcribe such statements of responsibility according to the applicable provisions of 2C.

2F. Publications without a collective title

When the title page bears the titles of two or more individual works contained in the publication, and one or more of these works has an edition statement associated with it, transcribe each edition statement in the title and statement of responsibility area along with the title to which it pertains.

> An examination of Dr. Burnet's theory of the earth ... / by J. Keill, The second edition
> corrected ... To the whole is annexed A dissertation on the different figures of coelestial
> bodies, &c ... / by Mons. de Maupertius

3. MATERIAL (OR TYPE OF PUBLICATION) SPECIFIC DETAILS AREA

No general use of this area is made for printed monographic publications. In using these rules to describe items that by their content fall within the scope of other portions of AACR 2 (e.g., an atlas), it is recommended that the provisions for this area in the appropriate section of AACR 2 be followed.

4. PUBLICATION, ETC., AREA

The name and location of the printer are here given equal status with the publisher and distributor. Thus the words "place of publication" and "publisher" refer equally to the location and name of a publisher, distributor, or printer, unless otherwise indicated.

Contents:
    4A. Preliminary rule
    4B. Place of publication
    4C. Publisher statement
    4D. Date of publication
    4E. Date of impression

4A. Preliminary rule

4A1. Punctuation

For instructions on the use of spaces before and after prescribed punctuation, see 0E.

Precede the publication, etc., area by a period-space-dash-space.

Precede a second or subsequently named place of publication by a semicolon, unless a linking word or phrase is given in the publication.

Precede the name of the first publisher by a colon. Precede the name of a second and any subsequent publisher by a colon unless a linking word or phrase is given in the publication.

Precede the date of publication by a comma.

Enclose the date of impression within parentheses.

4A2. Sources of information

The prescribed sources of information for the publication, etc., area are the title page, colophon, and other preliminaries, in that order of preference. If the information for an element (place, or publisher, or date) is not present in these sources, any source may be used to supply needed information, which is then enclosed in square brackets. This means that when statements belonging to the different elements are found in separate sources, they should be combined to make a complete publication, etc., area, with square brackets used as necessary. In general, do not combine statements belonging to a single element (place, or publisher, or date) when they appear in different sources within the publication (cf. 4C6 for an exception).

If any part of the publication, etc., area is taken from other than the title page, indicate its source in the note area. Give in the note area information not transcribed in the publication, etc., area if it is considered important.

4A3. Form of elements

Generally transcribe imprint information as it appears in the publication. Exceptions are provided in the specific rules.

4A4. Fictitious or incorrect imprints

When all the details of an imprint as given in the source are known to be fictitious or incorrect, nonetheless transcribe this imprint in the conventional order. If the real details about publication are known, supply them at the end of the area as a correction in square brackets. Give the source of this information in the note area. For any other case, apply the appropriate rule (cf. 4B9, 4C5, 4D2).

> Sadopolis : Chez Justin Valcourt ... à l'enseigne de la Vertumalheureuse, an 0000 [i.e.
> Brussels : Jules Gay, 1866]
> *Note:* Imprint from: Pia, P. Les livres de l'enfer

4A5. Imprints covered by labels, etc.

If any of the original details about publication are covered by a label or other means showing later information, give the later information. Give the original details in the note area.

4A6. Unpublished collections

For unpublished collections that group together publications with different imprints (e.g., miscellaneous pamphlets bound together) or collections of items of varying character only some of which are publications (e.g., a collection of pamphlets, broadsides, clippings, and maps), omit the place and publisher statements from this area and give only a date or span of dates. Use the note area to explain the date(s) selected or any other feature of the collection.

4B. Place of publication

4B1. Give the most prominently indicated (generally the first) place of publication, distribution, or printing as the place of publication. Transcribe it as found in the source of information used. If the place of publication appears together with the name of a larger jurisdiction (e.g., country, state, or similar designation), transcribe this as well. When supplying a place name, as opposed to transcribing it from a source, use an English form of name if there is one.

> Elizabeth-Town
> Köln
> Apud inclytam Germaniae Basileam
> Commonwealth of Massachusetts, Boston
> [Cologne]

4B2. Include in the transcription any prepositions appearing before the name of the principal place of publication, as well as accompanying words or phrases associated with the name.

> A Lyon
> In London
>
> In Boston, printed
> *(Title page reads: In Boston, printed. 1705)*
>
> Printed at Bennington
> Impressum fuit hoc opus Venetiis

4B3. If considered necessary for identification, supply in square brackets the modern form of the name of the place.

> Christiania [Oslo]

4B4. Supply the name of the country, state, province, etc., after the name of the place if it is considered necessary for identification, or if it is considered necessary to distinguish the place from others of the same name. Apply the abbreviations appearing in AACR 2, appendix B.

> Cambridge [Mass.]
> Newport [R.I.]
> Washington [Pa.]

4B5. If a place name is found only in an abbreviated form in the source, transcribe it as found, and add the full form or complete the name.

> Mpls [i.e. Minneapolis]
> Rio [de Janeiro]

4B6. If the source of information shows two or more places and all are related to the same publisher, record all in the order in which they appear. Do not, however, transcribe a second (or subsequent) place as a place of publication if it must be recorded as part of another element (cf. 4B8).

> London ; York
> A Lausanne & se trouve à Paris

If multiple places appear in more than one source, make a note for those not found in the particular source chosen for transcription of this element.

> Lugduni Batavorum
> *Note:* Place of printing in colophon: Trajecti ad Rhenum

4B7. When the publication is one issued in more than a single physical part, and the place of publication changes in the course of publication, give the place of publication of the later part(s) in a note.

> Stuttgart ; Tübingen
> *Note:* Vols. 33-40 have variant place of publication statement: Stuttgart; Augsburg

4B8. When the place of publication appears only as part of another area and is recorded there, or appears only as part of the publisher statement and is recorded there, add (in square brackets) the place of publication as the first element of the publication, etc., area. Use an English form of name if there is one.

> [Breslau] : Bey Caspar Closemann, Buchhandlern in Bresslaw zubefinden

4B9. When the place of publication given in the source is known to be fictitious or incorrect, add a correction in square brackets and give the basis for the correction in a note. If, however, a full imprint consisting of place, publisher, and date is fictitious, apply 4A4.

> Londres [i.e. Paris]
> *Note:* Actual place of publication from: Weller, E.O. Falschen und fingierten Druckorte

4B10. When no place of publication is given in the source, supply (in square brackets) as the place of publication the location of the most prominently indicated entity (publisher, distributor, or printer) or that of the first mentioned one. When there is doubt about prominence, prefer the location of the printer for 15th or early 16th century publications, otherwise that of the publisher or distributor. If the name of the place has changed over time, supply the name appropriate to the date of publication if possible, e.g., St. Petersburg (not Leningrad) for works published in that city before 1914. Provide a justification for the supplied place in the note area if necessary.

> [Cambridge, Mass.] : Printed by Samuel Green, 1668
> *Note:* The printer, Samuel Green, was located in Cambridge, Mass., from 1660 to 1672

4B11. Supply (in square brackets) the name of the place of publication when only an address or sign appears in the publication. (Record the address or sign within the publisher statement; cf. 4C4.) When supplying the place, give a justification in the note area if necessary.

> [Paris]
> *(Imprint reads: "à l'enseigne de l'éléphant," the trade sign of a Paris printer)*

> [London]
> *(Imprint reads: "sold in St. Paul's Church Yard")*

4B12. When the place of publication is uncertain, supply the name of the probable place with a question mark (all in square brackets).

>   [Amsterdam?]
>   [Newport, R.I.?]
>   [St. Petersburg?]

When no probable city of publication can be given, supply the name or the probable name of the state, province, or country as the place of publication, with a question mark if necessary (all in square brackets).

>   [Canada]
>   [Surrey?]
>   [Prussia?]

If, when supplying a place of publication, the reason for supplying the place is not apparent from the rest of the description, give in a note the source of such information.

>   Note: Place of publication suggested by Alden

When no place or probable place can be supplied, give the abbreviation "s.l." (sine loco), in square brackets.

>   [S.l.]

4B13. When the name of the place of publication appears in more than one language or script, give the statement in the language or script of the title proper, or if this criterion does not apply, give the statement that appears first. Use the mark of omission for statements omitted. Give the parallel statement in a note, if desired.

4C. Publisher statement

4C1. The publisher statement may include names of publishers, distributors, booksellers, and printers, together with associated information concerning places of activity and statements of printing and reprinting.

4C2. Transcribe the name of the publisher, together with any preceding words or phrases, as it appears in the publication. Generally omit addresses and qualifications such as "printer to the King." Addresses may be given, however, if they aid in identifying or dating the publication. Insignificant information in the middle or at the end of the publisher statement may be omitted. Indicate all omissions by the mark of omission.

If a statement such as "Privately printed" appears on the title page, record it as, or as part of, the publisher statement.

> : Printed for J. Warner
> : Chez Testu, imprimeur-libraire
> : J. Grundy, printer
> : Printed, and re-printed by E. Waters
> : Par Ian de Tournes pour Antoine Vincent
> : Impressit Gaspar Philippus pro Ioanne Paruo
> : Printed by John Baskerville for R. and J. Dodsley
> : Ex officina Ascensiana : Impendio Joannis Parui
>
> : Printed by Isaiah Thomas : Sold by him in Worcester, and by said Thomas and Andrews in Boston
>
> Imprinted at London ... : By Richard Tottel
> *(Title page reads: Imprinted at London in Fleetstreete within Temple Barre at the sign of the Hand and Starre, by Richard Tottel)*
>
> : Printed for the author and sold by J. Roberts
> : Printed for the editor, and sold by him
> : Privately printed

4C3. When the place of publication appears within the publisher statement, transcribe it as part of the publisher statement, even though it is also recorded in square brackets as the first element of the area, according to 4B8.

> [London] : Sold by T. Richardson in London
> [Breslau] : Bey Caspar Closemann, Buchhandlern in Bresslaw zubefinden
> [London] : Philadelphia printed, London reprinted for C. Dilly

4C4. When only the address, sign, or initials of the publisher appears in lieu of the name, transcribe the address, sign, or initials as the publisher statement. If the publisher's name can be identified, add this name using square brackets by filling in the name after the initials or by adding the name before or after the address or sign, as appropriate (cf. also 4B11).

> : [Costard] Rue Saint-Jean-de-Beauvais, la premiere porte cochere au dessus du College
> *Note:* Costard listed as printer in: Querard, J.M. La France littéraire
>
> : Prostant in Coemeterio D. Pauli [apud Abelem Swalle]
> *Note:* Publisher named on verso of t. p.

If the identification of the publisher is based on a device, substitute the name of the publisher in square brackets, even if the device includes the publisher's initials or spelled-out name.

Make notes as necessary about the basis for the identification, the source of the information used, the presence of the device, etc.

4C5. When the information given in the publication is known to be fictitious or incorrect, add a correction in square brackets and give the basis for the correction in a note. If, however, the full imprint is fictitious or incorrect, apply 4A4.

> : Par Mathurin Marchant [i.e. John Wolfe]
> *Note:* Printer identified in STC (2nd ed.)

4C6. If the publisher statement includes more than one publisher in a single source, generally transcribe all the names in the order in which they appear. Separate them with prescribed punctuation only when they are not linked by connecting words or phrases. If it is considered that the names are too numerous and that some may be safely omitted, shorten the publisher statement by omitting all the names after the first. In this case, use the mark of omission and add after it in square brackets a phrase in English to convey the extent of the omission.

> : Printed for J. Newbery, T. Becket, T. Davies, W. Jackson, in Oxford, and A. Kincaid,
> and Company, in Edinburgh

> [Pest] : Prostant Pestini apud authorem et Mauss bibliopolam ; Budae : Typis Leopoldi
> Francisci Landerer

> A Orleans : Chez Couret de Villeneuve ; Se trouve à Paris : Chez Nyon aîne ... [and 5
> others]

If multiple statements relating to publisher appear in more than one source, and one of these is the title page, prefer to transcribe in the publication, etc., area the statement on the title page. If one is a publisher statement and the other is a printer statement, transcribe both in the publication, etc., area if desired. In any case, make notes for any publisher statements not transcribed in the publication, etc., area.

> Lugduni : Apud Mauricium Roy & Ludouicum Pesnot
> *Note:* Colophon: Lugduni : Mathias Bonhomme excudebat

> London : Printed for Peter Parker
> *Note:* Colophon: Printed by R.W. for Peter Parker. Madan identifies R.W. as probably
> Robert White

> Imprime a Paris : Pour Galliot Du Pre marcha[n]t libraire ... : Par Maistre Pierre Vidoue
> *Note:* "Par Maistre Pierre Vidoue" from colophon

4C7. When the publication is one issued in more than one physical part and the name or form of name of the publisher changes in the course of publication, transcribe the publisher statement of the first or earliest part and give the publisher statement of the later part(s) in a note.

> : G.J. Göschen'sche Verlagsbuchhandlung
> *Note:* Vols. 8-10 have variant publisher statement: Verlag von G.J. Göschen

4C8. When no name, address, or device of a publisher appears in the publication, supply the name of the publisher (in square brackets) if known. When the responsibility of a publisher for a particular publication is uncertain or speculative, either add a question mark to any supplied name or give the information in a note. In any case of a supplied publisher, give supporting evidence in the note area.

4C9. When no publisher statement can be given, supply the abbreviation "s.n." (sine nomine) in square brackets.

> Paris : [s.n.]
> [S.l. : s.n.]

4C10. When the name of the publisher does not appear in the publication's imprint, but has already been recorded as part of another area, repeat it in the shortest convenient form within square brackets.

> [Paris : Symon Vostre, 25 Apr. 1500]
> (Philippe Pigouchet's device on title page. Title reads: Ces presentes heures a lusaige
> de Paris ... fure[n]t acheuees lan mil cinq ces le xxv iour dapuril pour Symon Vostre,
> libraire ...)

When a statement of publication is taken from the imprint, however, do not abridge or expand it because of its repetition or omission of information given elsewhere.

4C11. When the name of the publisher appears in more than one language or script, give the statement in the language or script of the title proper, or if this criterion does not apply, give the statement that appears first. Use the mark of omission for statements omitted. Give parallel statements in a note, if desired.

4D. Date of publication

4D1. General rule

The basic date for this area is the year of publication or printing. Transcribe this date from the publication, together with the day and month, if present.

> , 7th July 1766
> , 1732, reprinted 1734
> , 1482 le XII iour de may

Also transcribe words and phrases such as "printed in the year" and "anno" as part of this element. When both the place and the date of printing appear in conjunction with the phrase "printed in the year," ordinarily determine whether "printed" goes with the place or with the date according to the punctuation or typography of the source.

> London printed : [s.n.], in the year 1742
> *(Imprint reads: London printed, in the year 1742)*
>
> London : [s.n.], printed in the year 1742
> *(Imprint reads: London, printed in the year 1742)*

If the date is inseparably linked to data transcribed as part of another element or area according to one or more of the conditions enumerated in 1B1, transcribe it with the data to which it is linked and repeat it in square brackets as the date element of the publication, etc., area.

4D2. Transcription involving adjustments or additions

Roman numerals. When roman numerals appear as Gregorian or Julian years, change them to arabic numerals unless they are erroneous or misprinted.

> , anno gratiae 1614
> *(On publication: Anno gratiae MDCXIV)*

Transcribe years other than Gregorian or Julian as they appear.

> , an VII 1798
> *(On publication: An VII, 1798)*

Optionally, if it is considered important to retain in the catalog record the exact expression of the date, transcribe the date as it appears in roman numerals and add the date in arabic numerals in square brackets.

> , MDCLVI [1656]

Chronograms. If the date appears only in the form of a chronogram, give it in arabic numerals enclosed in square brackets and give the chronogram in the note area, if desired.

> , [1740]
> *Note:* Date of publication derived from chronogram: Ipso anno tertIo saeCVLarI typographIae DIVIno aVXILIo a gerManIs InVentae

Very long dates. If the statement of the date on the publication is very long, substitute for it a formalized statement in square brackets. In such cases, make a note concerning the source and the original form of the statement.

> , anno gratiae [18 May 1507]
> *(On publication: Anno gratiae millesimo quingentesimo septimo die vero decimoctavo Maij.)*
> *Note:* Date expressed in Latin words on t.p.

Fictitious or incorrect dates. When the year of publication or printing is known to be fictitious or is incorrect, transcribe it as it appears and add the real or correct year in square brackets. (If the full imprint is fictitious or incorrect, apply 4A4.)

> , DMLII [i.e. 1552]
> , 1703 [i.e. 1730]

If a date of printing from the title page has been recorded as the date element of the publication, etc., area, and evidence for a later date of publication appears in a source other than the title page, record the later date as a correction. If necessary, make a note to clarify that the date added as a correction is a differing date of publication, not a correction of an error on the title page.

> , 1786 [i.e. 1788]
> *Note:* On title page: 1786; in colophon: reprinted in 1788

Non-Christian-era dates, Roman-style dates, etc. For dates of the following types, add the equivalent date(s) in modern chronology, in square brackets if necessary: dates that are not of the Christian era; Roman-style dates; and dates that are in terms other than those of the calendar month. When adding dates in modern chronology, use the sequence: day, month, year.

> , shenat 627 [1866 or 1867]
> , an 7 [1798 or 1799]
> , Prid. Kal. Dec. [30 Nov.] 1488
> , Die visitationis Beatae Virginis Mariae [2 July] 1497
> , Die natalis Christi [25 Dec.] 1498

Non-Gregorian and Old Style/New Style dates.[6] When the year of publication or printing is based on a calendar in which the year does not begin on January 1, and the publication is known to have been published in the following year according to the modern calendar, add the later year in square brackets.[7] If the year of publication or printing is known to be an Old Style (i.e., Julian

---

[6] Information about the adoption of the Gregorian calendar from country to country, with tables for converting Julian ("old style") years to Gregorian ("new style") ones, may be found in AACR 2, footnote 18 to rule 22.17A, p. 414.

[7] For further assistance in establishing the modern date, consult a reference source such as Adriano Cappelli's *Cronologia e Calendario Perpetuo.*

calendar) date that needs to be adjusted, transcribe it and add the adjustment to New Style in square brackets, but without amending the month and day if present. In case of doubt, do not adjust the year.

> , Id. Mart. 1502 [15 Mar. 1503]
> , 1606 [i.e. 1607]

If two consecutive years appear as the publication date, representing both Old and New Styles of dating, transcribe both years, separated by a slash, and add the year according to the modern calendar in square brackets.

> , 1690/1 [i.e. 1691]
> , 169⁰ᴛ [i.e. 1691]
> , 1690/1691 [i.e. 1691]

Copyright dates.[8] Add the date of copyright following the publication date if it differs from the publication date.

> , 1967, c1965
> *(Copyright date printed on verso of t.p.)*

> , 1896, c1894
> *Note:* Publication date from verso of title page

4D3. When the date of publication or printing does not appear in the publication but is known, supply it in square brackets from any source, preferably a reliable bibliography or reference work, if possible. Give the source of a supplied date and any needed explanation in the note area.

> , [1876]
> *Note:* Publication date from BAL

4D4. Give the date of copyright as a substitute for an unknown date of publication or printing.

> , c1894

4D5. Give a conjectural date based on any information available. Give necessary indications of the basis for the conjecture in the note area.

---

[8]When applying this and other rules, use only copyright dates appearing in works published in a country after the enactment of modern uniform copyright legislation (in the United States, since 1870). A date of copyright that precedes the enactment of such legislation may be recorded in the note area, if desired.

Whenever the title page bears a prominent date that does not clearly represent the date of publication, either transcribe it as part of the title and statement of responsibility area or give it in a note.

> , [1814?]
> *Note:* At head of title: December 25, 1814
> *(Date at head of title is the date of the proclamation, not the date of publication)*

4D6. Give a probable date or period of publication according to one of the patterns shown in the examples below. Give any needed explanation in the note area.

, [1560?]	probable date
, [ca. 1580]	approximate date
, [ca. 1580?]	probable approximate date
, [not before 1479]	terminal date
, [not after 21 Aug. 1492]	terminal date
, [1727 or 1728]	one year or the other
, [between 1711 and 1749]	span certain
, [between 1711 and 1749?]	span uncertain
, [167-]	decade certain
, [167-?]	probable decade
, [16--]	century certain
, [16--?]	probable century

4D7. In describing a publication consisting of volumes, parts, or fascicles published over a number of years, give the date of the first published volume, part, or fascicle and the last published volume, part, or fascicle and connect them by a hyphen.

> , 1513-1524

If desired, give the date of each volume in a note. Such a note is particularly useful when the order of publication dates does not correspond to the order of the volume numeration.

> , 1560-1564
> *Note:* Vol. 1: 1561; v. 2: 1564; v. 3: 1562; v. 4: 1560

4D8. When parts of a publication have individual title pages bearing dates that differ from the date pertaining to the whole publication, give these additional dates in a note. If one of these dates is a more accurate reflection of the actual date of publication than the date pertaining to the whole publication, however, give it as a correction as instructed in 4D2.

4E. Date of impression

When a date of an impression later than the first is given in the publication and it differs from the date of publication transcribed as the date element, give the impression date in parentheses followed by the word "impression."

1786 (1788 impression)

When such a date of impression differing from the date of publication is known from a source outside the publication, give it in square brackets.

, 1786 ([1788] impression)

When the actual date of impression is known to differ from the date of impression given inside the publication, give it as a correction within square brackets.

, 1786 (1798 [i.e. 1789] impression)

In the above cases, the source of the date of impression and any explanations may be given in the note area if useful.

5. PHYSICAL DESCRIPTION AREA

Contents:
      5A. Preliminary rule
      5B. Extent
      5C. Illustration
      5D. Size and format
      5E. Accompanying material

5A. Preliminary rule

5A1. Punctuation

For instructions on the use of spaces before and after prescribed punctuation, see 0E.
Begin this area with a new paragraph.
Precede an illustration statement by a colon.
Precede the size by a semicolon.
Enclose a statement of format in parentheses.
Precede a statement of accompanying material by a plus sign.
Enclose physical details of accompanying material in parentheses.

5A2. Sources of information

Take information for this area from the publication itself.

5B. Extent

PUBLICATIONS IN ONE PHYSICAL UNIT

5B1. General

Give the complete number of leaves, pages, or columns in accordance with the terminology suggested by the volume (or other physical unit) itself. Describe a volume with leaves numbered on both sides, or with leaves unnumbered and printed on both sides, in terms of pages. Describe a volume with leaves numbered on one side only, or with leaves unnumbered and printed on one side only, in terms of leaves. When the leaves of a pre-1801 volume are numbered and printed on one side only, state this fact in a note. Describe in terms of columns a volume so numbered when it is printed with more than one column to the page. When a publication contains sequences of leaves and pages, or pages and columns, or leaves and columns, record each sequence in its appropriate terms.

Giving the "complete number" as stated above means giving the number on the last numbered page or leaf of each numbered sequence as the basic statement of extent, with any necessary additions according to succeeding rules, e.g., 5B3, for the addition of unnumbered pages or leaves. Give arabic and roman numerals as they appear in the publication. Give roman numerals uppercase or lowercase as they appear. When the pages or leaves are lettered rather than numbered, give the first and last letters followed by the word or abbreviation indicating pages or leaves. Use arabic numerals to designate pages, etc., that are numbered in words or in characters other than arabic or roman.

> x, 32 p., 86 leaves
> lxiij, [1] p.
> XII, 120 leaves
> 381 columns
> a-h p.
>
> 99 p.
> *Note: Pages numbered in words "one" to "ninety-nine"*

For the treatment of blank spaces on a folder or roll, see 5B15.

5B2. Normally imposed single sheets

For a normally imposed single-folded (i.e. 4-page) sheet, give the statement of extent in the same manner as for a volume. Apply this rule even if only one of the four pages is printed. See 5B14-5B15 for all other single-sheet publications.

5B3. Unnumbered pages or leaves

When unnumbered pages or leaves (printed or blank) are not included in a sequence of pagination or foliation, count them according to the terms used to describe the rest of the publication or the part of the publication with which they are associated. In ambiguous cases count them as leaves when they are all printed on one side only; otherwise generally count them as pages. Use arabic numerals within square brackets. Do not count possibly blank leaves wanting according to signature count and not known to exist in other copies. For works published before 1801 (and *optionally* for other works), include in the count blank leaves at the beginning of the first gathering or at the end of the final gathering when they are present in a copy in hand or known to be present in other copies.

> [8], 328 p.
> [2], 328, [6] p.
> iii, [1], 88 p.
>
> 64 p., [2], 16 leaves
> *(The unnumbered leaves introduce the following section)*
>
> 64, [4] p., 16 leaves
> *(The unnumbered pages are not closely associated with either adjacent section and one or more are printed on a verso)*

Consider that numbered sequences include unnumbered pages or leaves falling logically within the sequence, generally counting back from the recorded number to 1.

> [2], 40 p.
> *(Publication is numbered 3-40 and has four unnumbered pages at the beginning)*

Give in the following manner unnumbered blank pages or blank leaves interrupting a numbered sequence:

> 200, [8], 201-232 p.

If the number of blank pages or leaves is small, *optionally* supply a correction instead, as instructed in 5B7.

5B4. Errata leaves

Include errata leaves (but not errata slips) in the extent statement whether or not they are conjugate with another leaf of the publication. Mention the presence of errata leaves and errata slips in a note (cf. 7C16).

> 136, [2] p.
> *Note:* Errata on p. [137]

5B5. Advertisements

For pages containing only advertisements, make a concise mention of them in the statement of extent when they clearly belong to the publication. This is the case when they:

>   are included in the pagination;
> *or*   are printed on the pages of an initial or final gathering;
> *or*   are printed on a separate gathering issued within a publisher's binding;
> *or*   are known to be present in other copies.

If it is not possible to mention the advertisements concisely in the statement of extent, account for them in a note.

> 124 p. (p. 119-124 advertisements)

> 121, [3] p.
> *Note:* Advertisements on p. [1-3] at end

> 124, 8 p.
> *(Advertisements printed on continuously signed final gathering, or printed on a separate gathering issued within publisher's binding, or known to be present in other copies)*
> *Note:* Advertisements on p. [1]-8 at end

5B6. Multiple sequences of numbering

When the numbering within a sequence changes (e.g., from roman to arabic numerals), give each differently numbered part of the sequence.

> xii, 13-176 p.
> *(Publication is numbered [i]-xii, 13-176)*

When the publication has duplicate sequences of paging, as is sometimes the case with publications having parallel texts, give both pagings and make an explanatory note.

> xii, [1], 35, 35, [1] p.
> *Note:* Opposite pages bear duplicate numbering

When a volume has groups of pages numbered in opposite directions, as is sometimes the case with publications having texts in two languages, give the pagings of the various sections in order, starting from the title page selected for cataloging. If necessary, make a note clarifying the situation.

> ix, [1], 155, [1], 126, x p.
> *Note:* In English and Hebrew

When a volume has a pagination of its own and also bears the pagination of a larger publication of which it is a part, give the paging of the individual volume in this area and the continuous paging in a note.

> 328 p.
> *Note:* Pages also numbered 501-828

When the pages, leaves, or columns of a publication are numbered as part of a larger sequence (e.g., one volume of a multivolume publication) or the copy appears to be an incomplete part of a whole (see also 5B12 for incompleteness at end), give the number of the first and the last numbered page, leaf, or column. Generally precede the numbers with the word or abbreviation indicating pages, leaves, or columns.

> leaves 81-94
> p. 713-797
> (Fragments, detached from larger work)

> *But:*   [2], 713-797, [1] p.
> *(A complete publication, such as an offprint, issued separately with this pagination)*

When a publication contains more than three sequences of numbered or more than five sequences of numbered and unnumbered pages or leaves, preferably give all of the sequences. If it is not practicable to give all the sequences, then employ one of the following methods:

a)   Give the total number of pages or leaves followed by "in various pagings" or "in various foliations."

> 1024 p. in various pagings
> 256 leaves in various foliations

b)   When one of the sequences is clearly the main sequence, give the main sequence and the total number of other pages or leaves.

> 416 p., 98 p. in various pagings

c)   Give one of the designations used for publications issued in more than one physical unit (cf. 5B16).

> 1 v. (various pagings)

When one of these alternative methods is employed, *optionally* give all of the sequences in a note.

5B7. Expansions or corrections

When it is desired to give more precise information about pagination or foliation, blank pages or leaves, or other aspects of collation, either expand the extent statement (if this can be done succinctly) by adding information within parentheses after the statement of extent, or use the note area (see 7C10).

> 91, [1] leaves (the last leaf blank)
> 215 p. (p. [205]-[206] blank)
>
> vi, 744, [2] p.
> *Note:* LC copy: Several leaves are cancels; leaves page-numbered 105-106 and 539-540
> are cancellanda, with the corresponding cancellantia between p. 742 and p. 743

When the number of the last numbered page, leaf, or column of a sequence is incorrect, either give the number as given in the publication and supply a correction in square brackets or give the sequences exactly to indicate the source of the error. If desired, provide explanations in a note.

> xiv, 823 [i.e. 328] p.
> *Note:* Page 328 wrongly numbered 823
>
> 252 [i.e. 264] p.
> *Note:* Numbers 221-232 are repeated in pagination
>
> 232, 221-252 p.
> *(Same numbering as in preceding example)*

5B8. Lack of numbering

If the whole volume is unpaginated or unfoliated, count the pages or leaves and give the total in arabic numerals within square brackets. State the total in terms of pages or leaves, but not of both. Begin the count with the first page or leaf of the first gathering and end the count with the last page or leaf of the last gathering, as instructed in 5B3. Count all blank pages or leaves.

[104] p.
[88] leaves

5B9. Leaves or pages of plates

Give the number of leaves or pages of plates at the end of the sequence(s) of pagination or foliation, whether the plates are found together or distributed throughout the publication. Give the number even when there is only one plate. Count a double plate (a plate folded at the inner margin) as two leaves. Count unnumbered leaves or pages of plates without regard for the terms used to describe the rest of the publication (accordingly, leaves of plates may follow sequences of pages and pages of plates may follow sequences of leaves).

246 p., 24 leaves of plates

246 p., [12] p. of plates
(Plates are printed on rectos and versos of 6 leaves)

x, 32, 74 p., [1] leaf of plates
246 p., 38 leaves of plates, 24 p. of plates

When a volume contains a mixture of unnumbered leaves and pages of plates, give the number either in terms of leaves or of pages.

Treat tables printed on leaves that are not an integral part of any gathering as leaves or pages of plates.

Do not treat any illustrated title page (including an engraved title page) as a plate (cf. 5C1).

5B10. Folded leaves

Describe folded leaves as such.

122 folded leaves
230 p., 25 leaves of plates (some folded)

5B11. Double leaves

Count numbered double leaves (with fold at either top or fore edge) as pages or as leaves according to their numbering. Count unnumbered double leaves as pages (2 printed pages per double leaf) or as leaves (1 printed page per double leaf). Always indicate the presence of double leaves in a note.

[36] p.
Note: Printed on double leaves

[18] leaves
Note: Printed on 18 double leaves

5B12. Incomplete publications

When a volume or an individual sequence of pages or leaves within a volume lacks pages or leaves at its end — or an unpaginated or unfoliated volume or sequence lacks any pages or leaves — and the paging or foliation of a complete copy cannot be ascertained, give the number of the last numbered or unnumbered page or leaf followed by "+ p." or "+ leaves." Make a note of the imperfection.

xxiv, 178+ p.
Note: LC copy imperfect: all after p. 178 wanting

[8+], 237, [1] leaves
Note: LC copy imperfect: one or more prelim. leaves (incl. t.p.) wanting

5B13. Loose-leaf publications

For all loose-leaf publications that are designed to receive additions, give the number of volumes followed by "(loose-leaf)."[9]

1 v. (loose-leaf)

5B14. Sheets, rolls, cases, portfolios, etc.

For a publication in a single physical unit other than a volume (e.g., a sheet, a roll, a case, or a portfolio), use an appropriate designation ("sheet," etc.) preceded by the arabic numeral 1. When adding a statement of pagination or foliation, place it in parentheses following the designation.

1 portfolio (26 sheets)

---

[9]For more detailed guidance in cataloging looseleaf publications, consult Adele Hallam's *Cataloging Rules for the Description of Looseleaf Publications.*

5B15. Single-sheet publications

For a publication consisting of a single sheet designed to be used unfolded (whether issued folded or unfolded), add a statement of pagination based on the number of pages printed, generally not counting blanks, as follows:

> 1 sheet (2 p.)
> *(Sheet of any size printed on both sides, numbered)*
>
> 1 sheet ([2] p.)
> *(Sheet of any size printed on both sides, unnumbered)*
>
> 1 sheet ([3] p.)
> *(Folded sheet with title and colophon printed as 2 pages on "outside"; all text printed as one page occupying the entire "inside")*
>
> 1 sheet (1 p.)
> *(Broadside or other sheet printed on one side, numbered)*
>
> 1 sheet ([1] p.)
> *(Broadside or other sheet printed on one side, unnumbered)*

Describe a folder as follows:

> 1 folded sheet ([8] p.)
> *(A folder with 4 pages printed on each side of the sheet)*

Generally, do not count blank spaces on a folder or a roll as pages.

> 1 folded sheet ([5] p.)
> *(A folder with 4 pages printed on one side of the sheet and one page on the other side, which is three-fourths blank. If desired, the arrangement of printed and blank pages may be explained in a note)*

For a normally imposed single-folded (i.e. 4-page) sheet, see 5B2.

PUBLICATIONS IN MORE THAN ONE PHYSICAL UNIT

5B16. When a publication is issued in more than one physical unit, give the appropriate designation preceded by an arabic numeral indicating the number of such units. Exclude accompanying material from the numbering (see 5E).

> 3 v.
> 2 portfolios
> 6 sheets (versos blank)

When a publication has been issued in fascicles intended to be bound into one or more physical units, give the number of pages, leaves, or volumes appropriate to its final form, with a note indicating that it was issued in fascicles.

When the number of physical units in which a publication is bound differs from the number in which it was actually issued, state this fact in a note (see 7C18).

> 6 v.
> *Note:* LC copy bound in 3 v.

5B17. When the number of physical units in which a publication is actually issued differs from the numbering of the publication, state this fact in a note, unless the numbering of the publication is given in a contents note.

> 5 v.
> *Note:* Vols. numbered 1, 2A, 2B, 2C, 3

> 5 v.
> *Note:* The title page of the 5th vol. bears the designation "Bde. 5-8"

5B18. Use the term "pieces" as the designation for items of varying character (e.g., pamphlets, broadsides, clippings, maps) published as a collection, or assembled as a collection by the library. If desired, itemize or describe the pieces in the note area.

> ca. 6700 pieces
> *Note:* Pamphlets, broadsides, leaflets, manuscripts, photographs, etc., issued in several
> different countries

5B19. When the pagination of the publication in more than one physical unit is continuous, give the pagination in parentheses after the number of units.

> 8 v. (894 p.)

Do not use the physical description area to record preliminary sequences unless only the first volume contains such a sequence. A complete record of sequences may be given in a note.

> 3 v. (xx, 804 p.)
> *(Preliminaries are in v. 1 only)*

> 3 v. (804 p.)
> *Note:* Vol. 1: xx, 202 p.; v. 2: xx, 203-512 p.; v. 3: xxi, [1], 513-804 p.

5B20. When the pagination of a publication in more than one physical unit is not continuous, *optionally* give the pagination of each unit either in parentheses after the number of units or in a note.

> 2 portfolios (12, 18 leaves)
> 5 v. (32, 36, 48, 36, 18 p.)
> 3 v. (v, [1], 31, [1]; vi, 32; iii, [1], 49, [1] p.)
>
> 3 v.
> *Note:* Vol. 1: v, [1], 31, [1] p.; v. 2: vi, 32 p.; v. 3: iii, [1], 49, [1] p.

5B21. When a publication planned in more than one physical unit has been discontinued, or appears to have been discontinued, describe the incomplete set as appropriate (i.e., give paging for a single volume or the number of volumes for multiple volumes). Make an explanatory note.

> 2 v.
> *Note:* No more published?
>
> 627 p.
> *Note:* Vol. 2 was never published

5C. Illustration

5C1. To indicate the presence of illustration use the abbreviation "ill." *Optionally*, disregard minor illustrations. Do not regard illustrated title pages or ornaments (e.g., head-pieces, vignettes, tail pieces, printers' devices) as illustrations. Ornaments which are considered important may be mentioned in a note (see 7C10).

> 8 v. : ill.
> 492 p. : ill.
> 246 p., 32 p. of plates : ill.

Optionally, add the graphic process or technique.

> ill. (woodcuts)
> 30 ill. (metal cuts)

5C2. When they are considered to be important, specify particular types of illustrations. Use in alphabetical order one or more such terms as the following: coats of arms, diagrams, facsimiles, forms, genealogical tables, maps, music, plans, portraits (use for single or group portraits), samples. Replace the abbreviation "ill." with these terms if the particular types are the only illustrations in the publication.

> 492 p. : maps

Precede these terms with "ill." if the particular types are not the only illustrations.

> 492 p. : ill., maps, plans

5C3. Describe colored illustrations as such.

> col. ill.
> ill., col. maps, ports. (some col.)
> ill. (some col.), maps, plans

Do not describe hand-colored illustrations as colored unless there is evidence that the publication was issued with the hand-coloring. In either case, mention the hand coloring in a note (see 7C10 and 7C18).

5C4. Give the number of illustrations when their number can be ascertained readily (e.g., when the illustrations are listed and their numbers stated). Count an unnumbered illustration repeated in the publication as one rather than as two or more.

> 94 ill.
> ill., 8 facsims.
> 1 ill., 1 map

5C5. When some or all of the illustrations appear on the endpapers, make a note of this fact.

> ill., maps
> *Note:* The maps are on endpapers

5C6. When a publication consists entirely or mainly of illustrations, account for them with "all ill." or "chiefly ill." When the illustrations are all or chiefly of one type (see 5C2), use the name of the type instead of "ill."

> 518 p. : all ill.
> 518 p. : chiefly maps

5C7. Describe illustrations issued in a pocket attached to the publication in the illustration statement. Indicate the location, and when necessary clarify the number of illustrations in a note (cf. also 5E2).

> ill., 4 maps
> *Note:* The maps are in a pocket
>
> 12 maps
> *Note:* Four of the maps on 2 folded leaves in pocket

5D. Size and format

5D1. Give the height of a publication (based on the copy in hand) in centimeters exact to within one centimeter, counting a fraction of a centimeter as a full centimeter. When a publication measures less than 10 centimeters, give the height in millimeters.

> 18 cm.
> *(A publication measuring 17.1 centimeters in height)*

> 99 mm.
> *(A publication measuring between 98 and 99 millimeters in height)*

When a publication is bound, measure the height of the binding. When the height of the publication differs by 3 centimeters or more from the height of the binding, specify both.

> 12 cm. bound to 20 cm.

When a publication is unbound or inserted in a library binder, measure the height of the publication itself.

For publications issued before 1801, add the bibliographical format of the publication in parentheses following the size statement whenever the format can be determined. If desired, give the format also for later publications. Give the format in abbreviated form (fol., 4to, 8vo, 12mo, etc.; use 1 for volumes made up of unfolded sheets).

> 20 cm. (4to)
> *(A publication in quarto)*

> 20 cm. (4to and 8vo)
> *(A publication consisting of a mixture of quarto and octavo sheets)*

5D2. When the width of a volume is greater than the height or less than half the height, give the height followed by the width, separated by a multiplication sign.

> 20 x 32 cm.
> 20 x 8 cm.

5D3. When the volumes of a multivolume set differ in size, give the smallest or smaller size and the largest or larger size, separated by a hyphen.

> 24-28 cm.

5D4. When a volume consists of separate physical units of varying height bound together, give the height of the binding only.

5D5. Single-sheet publications

Give both the height and the width of a single-sheet publication issued unfolded. When a sheet is issued in folded form, but is designed to be used unfolded (e.g., with the chief part occupying a whole side of the sheet), add the dimensions of the sheet when folded.

1 sheet ([1] p.); 48 x 30 cm. folded to 24 x 15 cm.

When describing a folder (cf. 5B15), give the height of the sheet when folded.

1 folded sheet ([8] p.) ; 18 cm.

5E. Accompanying material

5E1. When a publication and its accompanying material are issued simultaneously (or nearly so) and are intended to be used together, give the number of physical units in arabic numerals and the name of the accompanying material at the end of the physical description.

272 p. : ill ; 24 cm. (8vo) + 1 price list

Optionally, give the physical description of accompanying material in parentheses following its name.

212 p. : ill. ; 21 cm. (8vo) + 1 atlas (38 p., 19 leaves of plates : col. maps ; 37 cm. (fol.))

272 p. : ill. ; 25 cm. (8vo) + 1 map (col. ; 65 x 40 cm.)

Alternatively, describe the accompanying material independently or mention it in a note (see 7C11).

5E2. When accompanying material is issued in a pocket attached to a publication, designate the location in a note. Do not treat illustrative materials in a pocket as accompanying materials (see 5C7).

6. SERIES AREA

Note that series statements are rare in early printed monographs and care should be taken to distinguish true series titles from other title information. When giving genuine series titles, see AACR 2.

7. NOTE AREA

Contents:
7A. General instructions
7B. Preliminary rule
7C. Notes

7A. General instructions

Notes qualify and amplify the formal description, especially when the rules for such description do not allow certain information to be included in the other areas. Notes can therefore deal with any aspect of the publication.

Notes, by their nature, cannot be enumerated exhaustively, but can be categorized in terms of the areas of description. In addition to notes relating to these areas, there are notes that do not correspond to any area of the formalized areas of description. Occasionally it may be useful to group together notes which refer to more than one area, for instance when they are all based on one source within the work, such as a privilege statement.

If the description in the areas preceding the note area does not clearly identify the edition or issue being cataloged, make whatever notes are necessary for unambiguous identification. When appropriate, refer to detailed descriptions in standard catalogs or bibliographies (see 7C14), or use both notes and references to catalogs or bibliographies.

Notes may also be made to justify added entries intended for special files of personal names, titles, genres/forms, physical characteristics, provenance, etc.[10]

Generally notes are not mandatory, but some notes are required in particular situations and are so indicated in previous rules, e.g., 1G3, 2A2, or 4A4, and in some of the rules for this area.

7B. Preliminary rule

7B1. Punctuation.

End each paragraph with a period or other mark of final punctuation. Do not use prescribed punctuation within a note, except in formal contents notes, "With:" notes, and notes of accompanying material that include the elements of the physical description area (cf. 7C11, 7C16, and 7C19). When formulating phrases or sentences in a note, use modern punctuation according to current good usage.

7B2. Sources of information

Take data recorded in notes from any suitable source. Square brackets are required only for interpolations within quoted material.

---

[10]Controlled vocabularies for such access points are available in various published thesauri (*Binding Terms*; *Descriptive Terms for Graphic Materials*; *Genre Terms*; *Paper Terms*; *Printing and Publishing Evidence*; *Provenance Evidence*; "Relator Terms for Rare Book, Manuscript, and Special Collections Cataloguing"; and *Type Evidence*).

7B3. Form of notes

Capitalization. Use uppercase or lowercase, according to the same practice applied to the title and statement of responsibility area.

Order of information. If data in a note correspond to data found in the title and statement of responsibility, edition, publication, physical description, or series areas, usually give the elements of the data in the order prescribed for those areas.

Quotations. Give quotations from the publication or from other sources in quotation marks. Follow the quotation by an indication of its source, unless that source is the title page.

> "Extracted from the minutes of the Society for the Propagation of the Gospel in Foreign Parts"

> "Generally considered to be by William Langland"--Harvey, P. Oxford companion to Engl. lit.

> "The principal additional music, contained in 72 pages, may be had, half bound, with or without the rules, price four shillings and ninepence"--Pref.

Formal notes. Use formal notes employing an invariable introductory word or phrase or a standard verbal formula when uniformity of presentation assists in the recognition of the type of information being presented or when their use gives economy of space without loss of clarity.

Informal notes. When making informal notes, use statements that present the information as briefly as clarity, understandability, and good grammar permit.

7C. Notes

A general outline of types of notes follows; other notes than those provided for may be made if desired. Specific applications of many of these notes are provided in the preceding sections. Make notes as called for in the following subrules, and, generally, in the order in which they are listed here. If a particular note is of primary importance, it may be given first, regardless of its listing here. When appropriate, combine two or more notes to make one note.

7C1. Nature, scope, or artistic form

Make notes on such matters when useful to amplify or explain the title proper and other title information.

> An advertisement
> A satire against William Pulteney
> Prospectus for: Pope's Essay on criticism. London, 1745

7C2. Language of publication; translation or adaptation

Make notes on the language of the publication, or on the fact that it is a translation or adaptation, unless this is apparent from the rest of the description.

> Parallel Iroquois and English texts
> English text with Latin and French prose translations
> Author's adaptation of his Latin text
> Translation of: Gulliver's travels
> In part a translation of: Le déserteur, by M.J. Sedaine
> Adaptation of: Breviarium monasticum

7C3. Source of title proper

Always make a note on the source of the title proper if it is from a substitute for the title page.

> Caption title
> Title from colophon
> Title from incipit on leaf [2]a

7C4. Variations in title

Make notes on titles borne by the publication other than the one chosen as the title proper. If desired, give a romanization of the title proper.

> Title on added t.p.: La naturaleza descubierta en su modo de ensenar las lenguas a los
> hombres ...
>
> Spine title: Bath Road acts
> Engraved t.p. reads: ...

If desired, also include here partial or complete transcription of title information to show the actual wording of the title page (e.g., when data have been omitted).

> Title page reads: ...

7C5. Parallel titles and other title information

Make notes on parallel titles appearing in the publication but not on the title page; also give other title information appearing in the publication but not on the title page if it is considered important. If parallel titles and other title information appearing on the title page have been omitted from the title area (e.g., because they could not be fitted into the body of the entry, or because they were very lengthy) they may be given here as notes.

> Title on added t.p.: The book of exposition = Liber rubens

> Subtitle: The medicinal, culinary, cosmetic, and economic properties, cultivation, and folklore of herbs, grasses, fungi, shrubs, and trees, with all their modern scientific uses

7C6. Statements of responsibility

Make notes to convey the following information:

1) **Authorship.** If the statement of responsibility transcribed in the title and statement of responsibility area appears in a source other than the recto of the title page, make a note to indicate this source.

> Author statement taken from verso of t.p.

If a statement of responsibility appears in the item but outside the sources for the statement of responsibility (cf. 1G2), give it and its source in a note.

> Dedication signed: Increase Mather
> Signed at end: A lover of truth

If no statement of responsibility appears in the item and facts relative to authorship are available, give this information in a note. Include the authority for the attribution whenever possible and useful.

> Published anonymously. By Cotton Mather. Cf. T.J. Holmes. Cotton Mather, 111
> Attributed to Jonathan Swift. Cf. H. Teerink. Swift (2nd ed.), 598
> Most of the pieces are either by or attributed to Voltaire. Cf. NUC pre-1956, v. 642, p. 47
> Translated by Peter J. de la Garza. Cf. hand-written card inserted in LC copy

If the statement of responsibility recorded in the title and statement of responsibility area or in a note is known to be fictitious or incorrect, make a note stating the true or most generally accepted attribution. Normally give the authority for the information.

> Preface signed: S.E.B. By Egerton Brydges; cf. Halkett & Laing (2nd ed.), v. 5, p. 276
> By John Locke. Author's name first appears on t.p. of 3rd and subsequent editions
> Introd. (p. xxix) refutes attribution to Petronius

"[Gregory King] was consulted about the coronation ... and was the principal author of the ... volume containing descriptions and splendid engravings of that ceremony ... though he allowed Francis Sandford to affix his name to the title-page"--Dict. nat. biog., v. 10, p. 131

"The identity of Junius, which he concealed with great skill, has never been definitely established ... He is now thought to have been Sir Philip Francis"--Drabble, M. Oxford companion to Engl. lit., p. 523
(The pseudonym "Junius" appears on the title page)

False attributions appearing in the bibliographical literature or in library catalogs may also be noted, along with the authority for the false attribution and the authority for questioning it.

Attributed to Daniel Defoe (cf. J.R. Moore. Defoe, 511); attribution challenged by: Secord, A.W. Robert Dury's Journal and other studies

2) **Other statements**. Give the names of persons or bodies connected with a work, or with previous editions of it, if they have not already been named in the description; give the authority for the information, if necessary.

At head of title: [name not used in the main entry heading and with indeterminate responsibility for the work]

Illustrations are woodcuts by Dora Carrington. Cf. B.J. Kirkpatrick. Virginia Woolf, A2a

Woodcuts on leaves B2b and C5b signed: b

3) **Variant names**. Give variant names of persons or bodies named in statements of responsibility if the variant forms clarify the names used in main or added entry headings.

By Gilbert Burnet, Bishop of Salisbury
(Statement of responsibility reads: by the Right Reverend Father in God, Gilbert Lord Bishop of Sarum)

By Charles Pigott
(Statement of responsibility reads: By the author of The virtues of nature)

4) **Transposed names**. Note here the original position on the title page of statements of responsibility that have been transposed to the title and statement of responsibility area.

On title page, editor's name precedes the title

7C7. Edition and bibliographic history

Make notes for the source of any element of the edition area when it is taken from elsewhere than the title page. Make notes for the original position of an element that is transposed to another position in transcription.

> The statement "corrected printing" from colophon
> The statement "amplified edition" precedes the title on title page

Make notes relating to the edition being described or to the bibliographic history of the work. In citing other works and other manifestations of the same work (other than different editions with the same title proper), give whatever information is appropriate, such as the title proper (or uniform title), statement of responsibility, edition statement, or date of publication. Arrange the information provided in the form that makes most sense in the particular case. (In citing bibliographies and catalogs, however, use the pattern for references to published descriptions shown in 7C14 whenever such a citation occurs in a formal "References:" note.)

> Revision of: 2nd ed., 1753
> Sequel to: Mémoires d'un médicin
> A reissue of the 1756 ed., without the plates
> Previous ed.: Norwich, Conn., Trumbull, 1783
> Sequel to: Typee
> Detailed description of plates in: Abbey, J.R. Travel in aquatint and lithography, 23

If a statement as to a limited number of copies of the edition appears, give this statement of limitation in a note, preferably in quoted form.

> "250 copies printed"--Pref.
> "Limited edition of 20 copies"--Verso of t.p.

When the statement of limitation includes the unique number of the copy being cataloged, give only the statement of limitation here. Give the copy number as a copy-specific note (cf. 7C18).

> Edition note: "Special edition of 200 copies on handmade paper"--Colophon
> Copy-specific note: LC has no. 20, signed by author

Alternatively, give the entire statement of limitation and the copy number as a copy-specific note.

7C8. Publication

Make notes on publication details that are not included in the publication area if they are considered to be important. When imprint elements have been taken from a source other than the title page, make a note specifying the source.

> Published in parts
> Publication date from Evans
> Imprint from colophon
> Publisher named in privilege statement as Sulpice Sabon
> Publisher statement on cancel slip. Original publisher statement reads: Sold by G. Walsh

Imprint judged to be false on the basis of printing of catchwords and signatures. Cf. A.H.
Sayce. Compositional practices, p. 116
No more published
"Copyright 1784"
Publication date from p. [4] of cover
At head of title: On the day of Lord Byron's death 1824

7C9. Signatures

Make a note giving details of the signatures of a volume, if desired. Give these details generally according to Gaskell's formula (cf. Gaskell, p. 328-332), insofar as typographical facilities permit. Preface this note with the word "Signatures" and a colon.

Signatures: [A]^4 B-C^4 D^2 E-G^4 H^2

For incunabula, it is generally desirable to give the signatures, especially if identical signatures are not given in a standard bibliographic source such as the *Gesamtkatalog der Wiegendrucke*, or the *Catalogue of Books Printed in the XVth Century Now in the British Museum* — as set out in 7C14.

If the gatherings are signed with one of the special characters used as abbreviation marks (cf. 0J2) but not permitted by available typographical facilities, substitute the spelled out form and enclose it in square brackets.

[rum]
[et]
[con]

If the gatherings are signed with other unavailable characters, substitute a descriptive term or an abbreviation for that term if a standard one exists.

[dagger]
(Gathering is signed with †)

[fleuron]
(Gathering is signed with ✌)

[par.]
(Gathering is signed with a paragraph mark: ¶)

[sec.]
(Gathering is signed with a section mark: §)

If typographical facilities for π and χ are not available, use the roman-alphabet forms "pi" and "chi" in the normal situation where they represent unsigned leaves (cf. Gaskell, p. 330). In order to avoid the impression that signatures printed with either the Greek or roman-alphabet forms are being accounted for, do not use square brackets. In the special situation where superscript π and χ are required to indicate partial duplication of an alphabet, and if typographical facilities are not available, substitute "[superscript pi]" and "[superscript chi]," the brackets added for clarity of the entire signature statement.

π^4 A-Z^4

pi^4 A-Z^4

$^\pi$A^4 A-Z^4

[superscript pi]A^4 A-Z^4

Alternatively, instead of making a note for signatures, make a note to provide a full collation.

Collation: 8vo: A-H^4; 32 leaves: p. [1-2] 3-62 [63-64]; $3(-H3) signed. H4 blank

7C10. Physical description

Make notes on important physical details that are not already included in the physical description area. For incunabula routinely and for later publications *optionally*, give the number of columns if more than one, number of lines, and type measurements if no account is found in a bibliographical source and the printer is unidentified or has been identified from this information. Give fuller details of the illustrations if these are considered necessary. Make a note on color printing if it is an important feature. Always note color printing in incunabula.

The first and last leaves are blank
24 lines; type 24G
Woodcuts: ill., initials, publisher's and printer's devices
Title and headings printed in red
Volumes numbered: 1, 2A, 2B, 2C, 3
Printed on vellum
Printed on a quarter sheet

Details of physical description given here usually apply to all copies of an edition or issue. If copy-specific information is noted, it should be given separately as described in 7C18 below.

7C11. Accompanying material

Make notes for any accompanying material not recorded in the physical description area. Give the location of accompanying material if appropriate.

Accompanied by: "Star guide" (1 sheet ; 12 x 36 cm.), previously published separately
in 1744

7C12. Series

Make notes on series data that cannot be given in the series area. If desired, give information about a series in which the publication has been issued previously, about series editors, or about other title information relating to the series.

> Editor of the series: ...
> Series t.p. reads: ...
> Originally issued in series: ...
> Also issued without series statement

7C13. Dissertations

If the publication being described is a dissertation or thesis presented in partial fulfillment of the requirements for an academic degree, give the designation of the thesis (using the English word "thesis") followed if possible by a brief statement of the degree for which the author was a candidate (e.g., "M.A." or "Ph. D.," or, for theses to which such abbreviations do not apply, "doctoral" or "master's"), the name of the institution or faculty to which the thesis was presented, and the year in which the degree was granted.

> Thesis--Harvard University, 1786
> Thesis (doctoral)--Universität Tübingen, 1805

If the publication is a revision or abridgement of a thesis, state this.

> Abstract of thesis--Yale University, 1795

If the publication lacks a formal thesis statement, give a bibliographic history note.

> Originally presented as the author's thesis (Universität Heidelberg) under title: ...

7C14. References to published descriptions

Give references to published descriptions, preferably in the form recommended by *Standard Citation Forms for Published Bibliographies and Catalogs* ... and "Citation forms for bibliographies appearing in journals ..." Accordingly, give references as illustrated below. Begin the note with the word "References" and a colon.

> References: Gaskell, P. Baskerville, 17
> References: Hiler, H. Bibl. of costume, p. 386

Give such references when available for all incunabula.

> References: Hain 6471; GW 9101; Goff D-403
> References: BM 15th cent., II, p. 346 (IB.5874); Schramm, IV, p. 10, 50, and ill.

For other printed materials, record a bibliographic citation whenever the edition being cataloged is listed in one of the following sources:

Blanck, Jacob. Bibliography of American Literature ...
(Cite in the form: BAL 2013)

Bristol, Roger P. Supplement to Charles Evans' American Bibliography ...
(Cite in the form: Bristol B1178)

Evans, Charles. American Bibliography ...
(Cite in the form: Evans 204)

Pollard, Alfred W. and Redgrave, Gilbert R. A Short-title Catalogue ...
(Cite in the form: STC (2nd ed.) 204)

Wing, Donald. Short-title Catalogue ...
(Cite in the form: Wing (2nd ed.) D204)

Cite any other list or bibliography when it would serve to distinguish an edition (or variant) from similar editions (or variants), when it would substantiate information provided by the cataloger, or when it would provide a more detailed description of the publication being cataloged.

References: Skeel, E.E. Webster, 408
References: Holmes, T.J. Cotton Mather, 111

7C15. Summary

Give a brief summary of the content of the publication if desired.

7C16. Contents

List the contents of an item, either selectively or fully, if it is considered necessary to show the presence of material not implied by the rest of the description, to stress items of particular importance, or to provide the contents of a collection or of a multivolume monograph. Note the presence of errata leaves and errata slips (cf. 5B4).

Transcribe contents from the title page if they are presented there formally and have not been transcribed as part of the title and statement of responsibility area. In such cases, follow the word "Contents:" with the parenthetical phrase "(from t.p.)." If a formal statement of contents is not present on the title page, take contents from the head of the parts to which they refer, or, if this is not feasible, from any contents list, etc., that is present. For publications in two or more volumes, generally transcribe the volume or part designations as found.

If a complete listing of contents cannot be assembled by one of the above means, the cataloger may devise a contents note from any appropriate source or combination of sources.

Includes bibliographical references (p. 43-58)
Includes bibliographical references
Includes index
"List of the author's unpublished poems": p. 151-158
Errata on last leaf
With an errata slip
Includes Joseph Pike's An epistle to the national meeting of Friends in Dublin

Contents: Love and peril / the Marquis of Lorne -- To be or not to be / Mrs. Alexander -- The melancholy hussar / Thomas Hardy

Contents: (from t.p.) I. The good housewife's coat of arms -- II. The spinning-wheels glory -- III. The taylor disappointed of his bride -- IV. The changeable world

7C17. Numbers borne by the publication

Make notes of important numbers borne by the publication other than those which can be associated with a series title.

7C18. Copy being described and library's holdings (Copy-specific notes)

Make notes on any special features or imperfections of the copy being described when they are considered important. Carefully distinguish such notes from other kinds of notes that record information valid for all copies of an edition. (For many older publications, however, it will not be readily ascertainable whether the characteristics of a single copy are in fact shared by other copies.)

Features that may be brought out here include rubrication, illumination and other hand coloring, manuscript additions, binding and binder, provenance (persons, institutions, bookplates), imperfections and anomalies, and copy number (cf. 7C7). For copy-specific "With:" notes, see the next rule.

Leaves I5-6 incorrectly bound between h3 and h4
Imperfect: leaves 12 and 13 (b6 and c1) wanting; without the last blank leaf (S8)

On vellum; illustrations and part of borders hand-colored; with illuminated initials; rubricated in red and blue

Contemporary doeskin over boards; clasp. Stamp: Château de La Roche, Guyon, Bibliothèque

Blind stamped pigskin binding with initials C.S.A.S.
Bound in batik by Joseph H. Howard
Signed in ms.: Alex. Pope
Formerly in the personal collection of William and Nina Matheson
LC has no. 20, signed by author
Newberry Library copy bound in 4 v.

7C19. "With:" notes

If the description is of part of an item that is made up of two or more separately titled parts that are also separately paged or foliated and have separate signatures, make a note beginning "With:" List the other parts of the item in the note, in the order in which they are found. In the case of bound volumes, list all the other parts on the record for the first part and, in general, only the first on the records for the subsequent parts. (Do not make such "With:" notes when the pagination, foliation, or signatures of separately titled parts are continuous with the part being described. Instead, record these titles in a contents note as instructed in 7C16.)

For each work listed give only the elements listed below:

a) the heading; normally give this element first, usually in catalog-entry form (e.g., with inversion of personal names under surname, but not necessarily including personal birth/death dates, corporate qualifiers, etc.);

b) the title proper as found in the record for the work; long titles may be shortened (whenever the uniform title is considered useful for the identification of the work, record it within square brackets preceding the title proper);

c) the primary statement of responsibility as found in the title and statement of responsibility area of the record for the work, unless it is redundant of the heading; and

d) the publication, etc., area as found in the record for the work, abridged as necessary.

> With: Dury, John. The reformed school. London : Printed for R. Wadnothe, [1650]

> With: The Bostonian Ebenezer. Boston : Printed by B. Green & J. Allen, for Samuel
> Phillips, 1698 -- The cure of sorrow. Boston : Printed by B. Green, 1709

If desired, add at the end of the note information to distinguish works issued together from works put together subsequent to publication.

> With: ... Probably bound together subsequent to publication [copy-specific]
> With: ... Bound together subsequent to publication [copy-specific]
> With: ... Issued together [universal]
> With: ... Probably issued together

If the works are too numerous to be listed in the "With:" note, make an informal note such as the following:

> No. 3 in a vol. with binder's title: Brownist tracts, 1599-1644.

8. STANDARD NUMBER AND TERMS OF AVAILABILITY AREA

If the publication bears an International Standard Book Number (ISBN) or an International Standard Serial Number (ISSN), see AACR 2 for giving the number. If it bears a price or other terms of availability and was published within the last three years, also see AACR 2 for giving such data.

Optionally, the "fingerprint" for older books may be recorded.[11]

---

[11]The Library of Congress will not determine or record the "fingerprint" for older books in its cataloging. For further information on this method of identification and on a recommended form of recording it, see *Fingerprints = Empreintes = Impronte* and *Nouvelles des empreintes = Fingerprint Newsletter*.

APPENDIX A: TITLE ACCESS POINTS

Preliminary notes

Under the present rules elements of information from a publication are generally transcribed as they appear, frequently without transposition or the other forms of intervention practiced by catalogers of ordinary books under AACR2. Title access then becomes an important means of making records for rare books as accessible as those in which transposition and other normalization occur. Certain characteristics special to early books provide another reason for special emphasis on title added entries: the imperfect state of many early printed books, including the absence of title pages or half titles, makes title access important for the location of copies in different institutions for purposes of identification and comparison. Finally, early practices in printing such as the use of older letter forms and contractions may result in problems of access for the modern researcher, and additional title added entries may resolve some of these problems.

The guidelines below provide explicitly for some of the specific situations that arise commonly from these rare book phenomena.

For examples and other matters, consult the rule cited in each guideline as well as the guideline per se.

General provision

Make an added entry for the entire title proper exactly as transcribed, omitting only an initial article as required. If the title proper is very lengthy, however, make an added entry for a version of it shortened by stopping at the first logical break after the fifth word.

Suggestions for certain specific additional title added entries follow; catalogers should select those most useful for the publication in hand.

0G. Misprints, etc.

If the cataloger has corrected the title proper in transcription, make an added entry for the title as it appears in the source, without the corrections. In addition, if a title proper has been corrected by the insertion of "[i.e. ...]" or "[sic]," make an added entry for the title as if it had been printed correctly.

If the title proper contains words spelled according to older or non-standard orthographic conventions, make an added entry for the title using the modern orthography.

0H. Forms of diacritical marks and letters (including capitalization)

Make an added entry for the modern orthography for a title proper in which I/J and U/V have been transcribed according to pre-modern conventions, when the modern version would differ from the title as transcribed. If necessary, also make an added entry for a form of the title in which all letters are transcribed as they appear in the source, but giving only initial letters in upper case. Generally, do not make an added entry using modern diacritical marks if this is the only difference from the title proper.

0J2. Special marks of contraction

Make an added entry for a title containing the cataloger's expansion of the contractions. If desired, also make an added entry for the title proper as it appears without the cataloger's expansion of the contractions.

0K. Initials, etc.

Make an added entry for a title containing initials, initialisms and acronyms with internal spaces between the initials, etc., and for the title without internal spaces.

1B1. Title proper

Make an added entry for a title proper inclusive of any preceding element that have been transposed elsewhere. If these preceding elements are not transposed, so that the title proper includes them, make an added entry for the chief title without these preceding elements.

1B3. Alternative titles

Make an added entry for an alternative title.

1B6. Supplementary or section titles

Make an added entry for a title that is supplementary to, or a section of, another work when both titles, whether or not grammatically linked, are recorded together as the title proper. If the supplement or section title is a title such as "Supplement" or "Chapter one," however, and so is indistinctive and dependent for its meaning on the main title, generally do not make the title added entry.

1E1-1E2. Titles of additional works

For other than supplementary matter, make added entries for the titles of additional works named on a title page without a collective title. Also, selectively make added entries for titles of additional works found in such a publication although not named on the title page.

1F1-1F8. Titles of works on single-sheet publications

Make added entries for titles of works on a single-sheet publication having a collective title. Also make added entries for titles of additional works on such a publication that does not have a collective title.

1G14. Titles or phrases about notes, appendices, etc.

Make added entries for titles or phrases concerning notes, appendices, etc., if the title or phrase is distinctive and the additional access seems required.

7C4-7C5. Title variants and other titles

Make added entries for cover titles, parallel titles, added title page titles, caption titles, half titles, running titles, and significant other title information.

7C11. Titles of accompanying material

Make an added entry for any separate title on accompanying material, if necessary for additional access.

7C18. Copy-specific titles

Make an added entry for copy-specific titles, such as binder's titles.

Conclusion

Although the list above represents those rules in DCRB that suggest situations in which the cataloger might profitably consider making a title added entry, it is not intended as an exhaustive list of all instances in which a title added entry might be required. Catalogers are urged to apply the principle of thorough access by title (cf. Preliminary notes) in dealing with situations not explicitly mentioned here.

APPENDIX B: EARLY LETTER FORMS

According to rule OH, earlier forms of letters and diacritical marks are usually converted to their modern forms. This appendix lists the most frequently occurring of these cases and provides advice in the cases that are special in some way. (For the treatment of the letters i/j and u/v, see the next section.)

ꝺ : appears at times with the vertical bar bent backward: transcribe it in its modern form (d)

ꝛ : appears at times roughly in the shape of the number 2: transcribe it in its modern form (r)

ſ : appears at times elongated: transcribe it in its modern form (s)

ligatures (ct, st, ß the double-s or scharfes-s, etc.): transcribe the letters separately, in their modern form (ct, st, ss, etc.). Exceptions are enumerated in rule OH

small e and o superscript over vowels: transcribe the e as an umlaut; transcribe the o as a small superscript circle, which is available in the MARC character set

This list is not intended to be exhaustive. The general advice should be followed for any case not mentioned: convert to the modern form if there is one; retain the older form when there is a special reason for doing so beyond ordinary fidelity to the source and the older form is available in the MARC character set.

Some knowledge of the history of printing as it applies to the letters i/j and u/v is helpful when applying the provisions of OH.

From the beginning of printing up to about the mid-17th century, the alphabet employed by printers commonly included i and j as simply two ways of printing the same letter: the understanding of these two forms as representing two separate letters is a modern development. The same is true of u and v; they were the two forms of a single letter. The uppercase employed by these printers usually included only the single capital letter I (in the form of a modern capital I in roman type, but more in the form of a modern capital J in italic or gothic type) and only the single capital V (in the form of a modern capital V in roman type, but more in the form of a modern capital U in italic or gothic type). The double V, in the modern form W, was absent from the alphabets used for Latin and romance languages. When the language being printed required its use, the printer employed VV in uppercase and vv or uu in lowercase. (It was often printed as a separate letter in blackletter texts in Germanic languages, including English.)

The use of the forms i and u for vowels and j and v for consonants is a distinction practically unknown in early printing. The printer usually selected the lowercase form of the letter, not by pronunciation, but according to conventional position within the word. The practice actually varies somewhat from printer to printer, but there were national or regional preferences for one pattern of practice or another. The practice of the individual printer can usually be discovered by an observation of the internal text (preferably in the same type as the title page) of the publication, and the clearest perception of these patterns is a natural by-product of handling the books and observing the conventions of the printers, book by book. In other words, the information provided here gives knowledge that will be only partially helpful; experience is the other, more essential teacher.

The following schema illustrates some patterns in printing and shows the cataloger's transcription on the basis of the particular pattern and is based on the example of two words printed in solid capitals in a title as IVS VERVM or as JUS UERUM:

Text	Pattern	Transcription
iuuenilia uerba Iulii	i & u always	ius uerum
iuuenilia verba Iulij	i initial & medial j final after i u medial v initial	ius verum
juvenilia verba Julij	j initial i medial j final after i u as vowel v as consonant	jus verum

A title page may include a word or words printed mainly in lowercase or small capitals but ending with a capital I, e.g., TiberI. This final capital I should be left in capital form and not converted to lowercase. Some printers occasionally employed the final single capital I, instead of ii or II, to indicate the genitive, vocative or locative case of a second-declension Latin noun or adjective with a stem in -io. Since this usage is not merely typographic but actually affects meaning, the capital must be left in that form.

Capital letters appearing apparently at random on a title page or colophon may represent a chronogram (see 4D2). These letters should be left in capital form and not converted to lowercase.

BIBLIOGRAPHY

Bowers, Fredson T. *Principles of Bibliographical Description*. Princeton, 1949, p. 162-163, 180-182. [1986 reprint: Winchester, U.K.: St. Paul's Bibliographies]

Cowley, J.D. *Bibliographical Description and Cataloguing*. London: Grafton & Co., 1939, p. 62-53.

Esdaile, Arundell. *A Student's Manual of Bibliography*. London: George Allen & Unwin & the Library Association, 1931, p. 259-261.

McKerrow, R.B. *An Introduction to Bibliography for Literary Students*. Oxford: Oxford University Press, 1927, p. 152-154, 310-312. [Available in various reprints]

McKerrow, R.B. "Some notes on the letters i, j, u and v in sixteenth-century printing." *The Library*, 3rd Series, no. 1 (1910), p. 239-259.

APPENDIX C: RARE SERIALS

This appendix is a revised version of the guidelines for treatment of rare serials published in the Library of Congress *Cataloging Service Bulletin* (CSB), no. 26, fall 1984. The CONSER Operations Committee and CONSER Operations Coordinator co-operated in making some necessary CONSER changes, most of which have been made in the *CONSER Editing Guide* (CEG). A few other changes have been made, indicated below with a statement of the CEG update number in which notification of the change has been published. (All the MARC format changes described in CSB no. 26 have been made in *USMARC Format for Bibliographic Data*.)

1. Cataloging Provisions

1.1. Apply the following cataloging rules to serials published before 1801 and to later ones for which a more detailed level of description is desired than is provided for by AACR 2:

> ---AACR 2
> ---Library of Congress Rule Interpretations (LCRIs)
> ---appropriate areas of DCRB, namely, 0-4 and 7.

When AACR 2 and LCRIs differ from DCRB, prefer DCRB, except as noted below.

Apply also the instructions found in the CEG.

1.2. Do not apply the provision of DCRB in 1B1 that allows for including within the title proper any other titles or statements about the chief title when they appear before the chief title on the title page. Instead, follow the approach to the selection of the title proper found in AACR 2. This will ensure that the national serials database shows consistency in choice of title for serials.

1.3. Transcribe serial designations in the form in which they appear in the source, in the numeric and/or alphabetic, chronological, or other designation area. If these elements are grammatically linked to one or more elements in the title and statement of responsibility area, use the mark of omission in that area to indicate their omission.

1.4. Apply the principle that information from any source other than the prescribed source of information is enclosed in square brackets.

1.5. When appropriate, add the bibliographic format in the physical description area, as provided for in DCRB 5D1.

1.6. Whenever possible, give references to published descriptions in the note area, following DCRB 7C14. (See also 2.3 below.)

1.7. Apply liberally the provisions for making notes found in AACR 2 12.7 and in DCRB area 7. For rare serials it is often important to expand the use of notes to bring out specific points, e.g., certain contributors, illustrators, etc. (See also 2.4 below.)

1.8. When considered desirable by the cataloging institution, create separate records for individual issues of a serial in addition to the collective record for the entire serial. Link the individual records to the collective record by whichever technique is available or preferred by the institution (see also 2.8

below). This allows detailed bibliographic description of single issues of rare and early serials, together with subject analysis pertinent to each issue separately cataloged, which is particularly important in the case of rare serials for which extant issues are sparse.

1.9. Use "designations of function" ("relator terms") when appropriate to the publication being cataloged or when required by institutional policy, as provided in AACR 2 21.0D and in *Relator Terms for Rare Book, Manuscript, and Special Collections Cataloguing.*[12] (See also 2.9 below.)

2. MARC Format Provisions

Use the following MARC content designators, as appropriate, in CONSER/national level serial records:

2.1. Subfield ǂe in the 040 field: use the code "dcrb."

2.2. Subfield ǂ5 in the 500, 700, 710, 711, 730, and 740 fields (This allows the careful identification and communication of copy specific information in MARC serial records.)

2.3. Field 510, 1st indicator values 3 and 4 (This allows the inclusion of references to published descriptions for serial records in a field specifically defined for them.)

2.4. Field 570 (This allows the inclusion of information regarding editors, compilers, illustrators, or translators of serials in a field specifically defined for them.)

2.5. Field 655 (This allows the inclusion of genre/form headings in serial records to enhance access.)

2.6. Field 752 (This allows additional access to rare serials by hierarchical place names.) Instructions for the use of this field permit use of the field for rare serials, according to CEG Update 7.

2.7. Field 755 (This allows the inclusion of access terminology relating to the physical aspects of the serial.) This field is defined in the CEG Update 7.

2.8. Field 772 (*Optionally*, this field is used in a record for an individual issue of a serial to link it back to the collective record.) Instructions and an example may be found in CEG Update 7, which advises that the first indicator position be set <u>not</u> to print a note "Supplement to."

2.9. Subfield ǂe in fields 700 and 710. (This allows the use of relator terms or designations of function in serial records.)

2.10. Subfield ǂ4 in fields 700/710/711. (This allows the use of relator codes in serial records, for those libraries preferring them to the textual relator terms.)

---

[12]Cf. also *USMARC Code List for Relators, Sources, Description Conventions.*

3. Individual issues of serials

3.1. Guidelines 1.8 and 2.8 above refer to the possibility of preparing both a collective record for the entire serial and separate records for individual issues. The additional guidelines below are provided to address the situation in which the institution desires separate records for individual issues, either instead of, or in addition to, a record for the serial as a whole.

3.2. Bibliographic level. The bibliographic level for individual issues of serials is "m" (monograph), just as it is for an individual part of a multipart item cataloged separately.

3.3. Transcription of body of description. Formulate the description according to the rules for transcription from monographs, except for using the sources of information applicable to serials. Follow the special rules in DCRB for full and exact transcription of bibliographic information. Following AACR 2 and ISBD conventions, transcribe the date of publication and volume designation as the "number of part" and transcribe any special issue title as "name of part."

> The Post boy. Numb. 2436, from Thursday December 21 to Saturday December 23, 1710

> Hollandia : a weekly paper for Dutchmen abroad. Special Transvaal-number : bijvoegsel behoorende bij het nummer van 2 September 1899 / written and edited by L. Simons

> The Foundling hospital for wit : intended for the reception and preservation of such brats of wit and humour whose parents chuse to drop them. Number III, to be continued occasionally / by Timothy Silence, Esq.

For MARC coding of title elements, follow the existing conventions for monographs.[13] (This may result in some apparent inconsistency in content designation of individual issues of the same serial if the chief sources of information vary in their placement of the elements; this inconsistency, however, is unavoidable and of little consequence, since it is the added entry for the collective title that can provide organized, sequential access to records for issues of a serial.)

> 245 04 ‡a The Post boy. ‡n Numb. 2436, from Thursday December 21 to Saturday December 23, 1710

> 245 00 ‡a Hollandia : ‡b a weekly paper for Dutchmen abroad. Special Transvaal-number : bijvoegsel behoorende bij het nummer van 2 September 1899 / ‡c written and edited by L. Simons

> 245 14 ‡a The Foundling hospital for wit : ‡b intended for the reception and preservation of such brats of wit and humour whose parents chuse to drop them. Number III, to be continued occasionally / ‡c by Timothy Silence, Esq.

---

[13]Note that according to LC MARC editing conventions, subfields ‡n and ‡p of field 245 are assigned only when the number and name of part elements directly follow subfield ‡a.

3.4. Relating records for individual issues to the serial as a whole. If it is desired to relate the records for individual issues to the serial as a whole or to provide organized access to the records in a file, make an added entry under the name of the serial, following the conventions for series added entries. Apply AACR 2 and the LCRIs in formulating the uniform title for the serial. Normalize the numeration of the individual issues, as is done for monographic series.

> 830 ⱷ0 ‡a Post boy (London, England) ; ‡v no. 2436
> 830 ⱷ0 ‡a Hollandia (Hague, Netherlands)
> 800 1ⱷ ‡a Silence, Timothy. ‡t Foundling hospital for wit ; ‡v no. 3

If the serial has a chronological designation but no actual enumeration, use a standardized form of the chronological designation in the access point.

> 245 04 ‡a The English Lucian, or, Weekly discoveries of the witty intrigues, comical
> passages, and remarkable transactions in town and country, with reflections on the
> vices and vanities of the times. ‡n Friday the 17th of January, 1698
>
> 830 ⱷ0 ‡a English Lucian ; ‡v 1698 Jan. 17

3.5. Linkage of records for individual issues to the collective record for the serial. If desired, link records for individual issues to the serial title by a 772 "Parent Record Entry" field.

> 772 1ⱷ ‡7 unas ‡a Post boy (London, England). ‡w (OCoLC) 1234567
> 772 1ⱷ ‡7 plas ‡a Silence, Timothy. ‡t Foundling hospital for wit. ‡w (DLC) 85-14367

If a linking entry is desired, include the AACR 2 heading for the serial and the record number of the related record for the serial as a whole.

APPENDIX D: MINIMAL-LEVEL RECORDS

The elements of description provided in DCRB constitute a full set of information for describing rare materials. This appendix sets out a less full level of description containing those elements recommended as a minimum for effective description of early printed books and other rare materials.

Libraries base their choice of a level of description on the purpose of the catalog or catalogs for which an entry is constructed. In selecting DCRB for describing rare materials, libraries make the decision that a more detailed, transcription-oriented description is warranted.

Libraries most often turn to minimal-level cataloging for rare materials in response to a need to create machine-readable records for large backlogs of uncataloged or manually cataloged materials with the least amount of time and effort possible. These guidelines are provided in response to such needs; their purpose is not to promote the use of DCRB minimal-level cataloging, but rather to provide a usable standard for those institutions wishing to adopt it.

A minimal-level cataloging policy is best kept simple. Complex rules for omitting or shortening a variety of record elements would require catalogers to devote time to learning these new rules, thereby eliminating a portion of the intended gains in time and expense. In addition, tampering with the full description provided by DCRB areas 0-6 and 8 would negate the very purpose of using DCRB for description of rare materials. The conclusion then is that eliminating notes accomplishes much of the purpose of minimal-level cataloging because it saves considerable time while not unduly limiting access. Bibliographic records following this approach will, in most cases, still identify the books being described and distinguish them from similar editions or issues.

1. Follow the rules in DCRB areas 0-6 and 8. In general, abridge the description wherever possible as allowed by the rules. Do not make the mandatory notes found in areas 0-6, such as those called for in rules 2A2, 2C2, 4A4, etc. For the notes called for in rules 7A-7C19, do not make them routinely but only when especially necessary.

2. *Optionally*, libraries may add any additional elements in accordance with institutional policy, and may wish in particular to consider adding one or more of the following, each of which would significantly enhance the value of minimal-level DCRB records for identifying rare materials.

—references to published descriptions in standard bibliographies (rule 7C14), particularly when the source cited provides more detailed information than the minimal-level catalog record;

—the mandatory notes called for in DCRB (rules 2C2, 4A2, etc.);

—one or more copy-specific notes describing provenance, copy numbering, imperfections, binding, or any other information that will allow the bibliographic record to describe the particular copy in hand with sufficient precision to indicate the institution's ownership of that particular copy;

—optional note regarding transposition of elements in areas 1-4 of the description (rules 2B7, 2C3, etc.);

—optional notes based on reliable dealers' descriptions accompanying the item being described.

3. Minimal-level cataloging policies often eliminate or simplify additional areas of the catalog record such as subject headings, classification, or other access points. Users of DCRB may also wish to streamline these areas according to local needs, taking into consideration the effect that such policies will have on special files for printers, binders, bindings, genres, provenance, and the like.

APPENDIX E: DCRB CODE FOR RECORDS

General. Under certain circumstances, USMARC field 040, subfield ǂe, is used to indicate, by means of a code, the descriptive cataloging rules followed in cataloging an item. This appendix offers guidance in using "dcrb," the code designating DCRB. Usually, the brief statements provided in bibliographic network documentation suffice, i.e., use this code when DCRB is used as the descriptive cataloging convention. Some cases, however, require further clarification, particularly when the material being cataloged is not an early printed book or when the record being created varies in some aspect from that of a full-level, standard AACR 2/DCRB record commonly created by the Library of Congress.

It is important to understand the purpose of indicating the descriptive cataloging rules followed: to identify those records that exemplify descriptive cataloging conventions <u>other</u> than those called for in AACR 2, AACR 1, ALA 1949, ALA 1941, or ALA 1908. The code then is primarily an aid to catalogers in recognizing those instances when specialized descriptive cataloging rules have been used. The fact that a record is coded "dcrb" should not be interpreted as necessarily indicating a "higher" level of cataloging; instead, it is merely an indication that the specialized rules developed to accommodate the needs of rare book cataloging have been used.

1. Minimal-level DCRB. Apply the code "dcrb" to records for items cataloged according to the minimal-level guidelines found in Appendix D. The fact that such records exemplify the minimal-level version of DCRB is stated by the value assigned in the encoding level for minimal-level cataloging and the code "dcrb" in 040 subfield ǂe. Do not use "dcrb" for cataloging based on AACR 2's Level 1 or on any other minimal-level standard.

2. Microforms of early printed books. Apply the code "dcrb" to records for microforms in which the descriptive portion of the record exemplifies DCRB (full level or minimal level). If, however, DCRB (full or minimal level) is not used in all aspects but instead in some "hybrid" fashion, do not use "dcrb."

3. Rare serials. Apply the code "dcrb" to rare serials when they are cataloged according to the guidelines found in Appendix C.

4. Nonbook formats. Do not apply the code "dcrb" to records for nonbook materials such as maps, music, and graphics even though they may have been cataloged according to an adapted, "DCRB-like" standard.

5. "Special collections cataloging." In this context "special collections cataloging" means fuller use of notes, access points, and other elements that are not specifically called for in AACR 2 or its predecessors, but that follow the spirit of DCRB without following its rules completely. Such cataloging is frequently done for 19th and 20th century materials housed in special collections. Do not apply the code "dcrb" to records for "special collections cataloging" unless the cataloging follows DCRB completely (full level or minimal level). In many cases, the way the extent of the item is recorded (DCRB rules 5B1-5D5 or AACR 2 rules 2.5B-2.5D) will provide the clearest indication of whether DCRB has actually been used or whether the record represents "special collections cataloging."

APPENDIX F: CONCORDANCE BETWEEN RULES IN DCRB AND AACR 2

This concordance shows the relationships between specific rules in DCRB and the 1988 revision of AACR 2.

Both chapters 1 and 2 of AACR 2 were used in compiling the concordance, since some DCRB rules correspond only to rules in chapter 1, others only to chapter 2. Not considered were the rules for areas 3, 6, and 8, for which there are no rules in DCRB.

For the most part, there is a one-to-one correspondence between each DCRB rule and a rule in AACR 2. Rules that match each other "in spirit" were considered a one-to-one match. Several DCRB rules (e.g., 1F1-1F8), however, have no equivalent in AACR 2. The phrase "nothing comparable" is used in these cases.

DCRB	AACR2
0. GENERAL RULES	
0A	2.12A
0B1	1.0D
0B2	1.0A
0C1	2.0B1, 2.13A
0C2	1.0H
0C3	1.0A2, 2.0B1, 2.14A
0D	2.0B2
0E	1.0C1
0F	1.0E1
0G	1.0F1
0H	1.0G1, 2.14E
0J1	1.0E1, appendix B.4A
0J2	1.0C1
0K	1.1B6

DCRB	AACR2
1. TITLE AND STATEMENT OF RESPONSIBILITY AREA	
1 contents	1.1
1A1	1.1A1
1A2	1.1A2, 2.14C
1B1	1.1B1
1B2	1.1B1
1B3	1.1B2, 1.1B3
1B4	1.0H2
1B5	1.1B7, 2.14A
1B6	1.1B9
1B7	1.1B4, 2.14B
1C	1.1D1, 1.1D3
1D1	1.1E2
1D2	2.14D
1D3	Nothing comparable
1D4	1.1E3, 2.14F

DCRB	AACR2
1D5	1.1E4
1D6	1.1E5
1E1	1.1G3
1E2	1.0H1a, 1.1G3
1F	Nothing comparable
1G1	1.1F1
1G2	1.1F2
1G3	1.1F3
1G4	1.1F4
1G5	1.1F5
1G6	1.1F6
1G7	1.1F7
1G8	1.1F7
1G9	1.1F8
1G10	1.1F10
1G11	1.1F12
1G12	1.1F14
1G13	Nothing comparable
1G14	Nothing comparable

DCRB	AACR2
2. EDITION AREA	
2 contents	1.2
2A1	1.2A1
2A2	1.2A2
2B1	1.2B1, 2.15A
2B2	1.2D3
2B3	1.2B3
2B4	1.2B2
2B5	1.2B4
2B6	1.1B2, 2.15B
2B7	Nothing comparable
2B8	Nothing comparable
2B9	1.2B5
2C1	1.2C1

DCRB	AACR2
2C2	1.2C2
2C3	Nothing comparable
2D1	1.2D1
2D2	Nothing comparable
2D3	1.2D3
2E1	1.2E1
2E2	1.2E1
2F1	1.2B6

4. PUBLICATION, ETC., AREA

DCRB	AACR2
4 contents	1.4
4A1	1.4A1
4A2	1.4A2
4A3	Nothing comparable
4A4	1.4B6
4A5	1.4B5
4A6	1.4C8, 1.4D9, 1.4F10
4B1	1.4C1, 2.16B
4B2	Nothing comparable
4B3	1.4C2, 2.16B
4B4	1.4C3
4B5	1.4C4
4B6	2.16C
4B7	1.0H2
4B8	Nothing comparable
4B9	1.4B6
4B10	Nothing comparable
4B11	Nothing comparable
4B12	1.4C6
4B13	1.4C1
4C1	2.16A
4C2	2.16D
4C3	Nothing comparable
4C4	Nothing comparable
4C5	1.4B6
4C6	2.16E
4C7	1.4D5
4C8	Nothing comparable
4C9	1.4D7
4C10	1.4D4
4C11	1.4D2
4D1	2.16F
4D2	1.4F1, 1.4F5, 2.16F
4D3	Nothing comparable
4D4	1.4F6
4D5	1.4F7
4D6	1.4F7

DCRB	AARC2
4D7	1.4F8
4D8	Nothing comparable
4E	1.4G4

5. PHYSICAL DESCRIPTION AREA

DCRB	AARC2
5 contents	1.5
5A1	1.5A1
5A2	1.5A2
5B1	2.5B1, 2.17A1
5B2	Nothing comparable
5B3	2.5B3, 2.17A1
5B4	Nothing comparable
5B5	2.5B3
5B6	2.5B5, 2.5B6, 2.5B8, 2.5B13, 2.5B14, 2.5B15
5B7	2.5B4
5B8	2.5B7
5B9	2.5B10
5B10	2.5B11
5B11	2.5B12
5B12	2.5B16
5B13	2.5B9
5B14	2.5B18
5B15	Nothing comparable
5B16	2.5B17
5B17	2.5B19
5B18	2.5B18
5B19	2.5B20
5B20	2.5B21
5B21	2.5B22
5C1	2.5C1, 2.17B1
5C2	2.5C2
5C3	2.5C3, 2.17B1
5C4	2.5C4
5C5	2.5C5
5C6	2.5C6
5C7	2.5C7
5D1	2.5D1, 2.17C1
5D2	2.5D2
5D3	2.5D3
5D4	2.5D5
5D5	2.5D4
5E1	1.5E1
5E2	2.5E2

DCRB	AACR2

7. NOTE AREA

7 contents	1.7
7A	2.18A
7B1	1.7A1
7B2	1.7A2
7B3	1.7A3
7C	1.7A5, 1.7B
7C1	2.7B1
7C2	2.7B2
7C3	2.18B1
7C4	2.7B4
7C5	2.7B5
7C6	2.7B6
7C7	2.7B7
7C8	2.7B9
7C9	2.18D1
7C10	2.7B10, 2.18E1
7C11	2.7B11
7C12	2.7B12
7C13	2.7B13
7C14	2.18C1
7C15	2.7B17
7C16	2.7B18
7C17	2.7B19
7C18	2.7B20, 2.18F1
7C19	2.7B21

APPENDIX G: GLOSSARY

This glossary is intended to supplement the glossary in AACR 2, appendix D. The terms included here are either lacking in AACR 2, or, though present there, require some amendment to accommodate these rules for the description of special printed materials. The definitions marked with an asterisk have been taken from G. Thomas Tanselle's "The bibliographical concepts of issue and state," in *The Papers of the Bibliographical Society of America*, 69 (1975), p. 17-66.

Bibliographic description. A set of bibliographic data recording and identifying a publication, excluding access points, i.e., the description that begins with the title proper and ends with the last note in the note area.

Broadside, broadsheet. *See* **Single-sheet publication.**

Chief title. The distinguishing word or sequence of words that names a publication, as given on the title page (or substitute). This definition excludes alternative titles, parallel titles, other title information, and subsidiary title information preceding the chief title on the title page, such exclusion resulting usually in a short title. *See also* **Title proper.**

*Edition. All copies resulting from a single job of typographical composition.

Fingerprint. A group of characters taken from the text of the publication, which, with the addition of an imprint date and an edition or impression number, may serve to identify the publication uniquely.

Folder. A sheet other than a normally imposed single-folded sheet, folded into four or more numbered or unnumbered pages so imposed that they are to be read in sequence when the sheet is unfolded.

Illustration. A pictorial, diagrammatic, or other graphic representation occurring within a publication.

Impression. All copies produced in the frame of one printing event; the term is synonymous with "printing."

*Issue. A group of published copies of an impression which constitutes a consciously planned publishing unit, distinguishable from other groups of published copies of that impression by one or more differences designed expressly to identify the group as a discrete unit.

Leaf of plates. A plate in a publication that also has one or more leaves of text (whether preliminary leaves or text proper). Leaves of plates may be described in terms of pages of plates if they are numbered as pages or are unnumbered and have illustrative matter on both sides. *See also* **Plate.**

Plate. A primarily illustrative leaf that is not an integral part of a gathering, excepting an illustrated title page (including half title and added title page). Tables printed on leaves that are not an integral part of a gathering are also treated as plates, unlike other textual leaves, which are excluded from consideration as plates. *See also* **Leaf of plates.**

Single-sheet publication. A publication printed on a single or composite piece of paper or other material; it may be printed on one or both sides and may be bound or unbound. The content of a single-sheet publication, as here defined, is predominantly textual in nature, though it may contain illustrations that are subordinate or coordinate to the text. (See 5B2 for normally imposed single sheets and 5B15 for single sheets designed to be read unfolded.) *See also* **Folder**.

*State. A copy or a group of copies of a printed sheet or a publisher's casing which differs from other copies (within the same impression or issue) of that sheet or casing in any respect which the publisher does not wish to call to the attention of the public as representing a discrete publishing effort.

Title page. The leaf on which the chief title appears. When used in reference to "chief source of information" and "prescribed sources of information," "title page" refers only to the recto of the leaf. (The verso of this leaf is not a part of the "title page"; instead it is one of the "preliminaries." Cf. the definition of "preliminaries" in the AACR 2 Glossary.) *See also* **Title proper**.

Title proper. The chief title of a publication in the form in which it appears on the title page (or substitute), along with any alternative title or any other titles or title information appearing ahead of the chief title on the title page. This definition excludes parallel titles and other title information following the chief title as well as such elements as the following when they are not grammatically linked to the title proper: statements of responsibility, edition statements, statements pertaining to the publication, etc., of an item, series statements, prices, pious invocations, devices, announcements (including epigrams and dedications), mottoes, statements of patronage, and other information that cannot be considered part of the title of the publication. For publications containing several individual works, the title proper is the collective title. The title proper of publications containing several individual works and lacking a collective title is the group of titles of the individual works named in the chief source. *See also* **Chief title**.

Variant. A copy showing any bibliographically significant difference from one or more other copies of the same edition. The term may refer to an impression, issue, or state.

INDEX

A

AACR 2, 0A, App. A
 abbreviations, 4B4
 concordance between DCRB and, App. F
 in serials cataloging, App. C
 rules for series, 6
Abbreviations
 expansion, 0J2
 general rules, 0J
 in edition statement, 2B1, 2B4
 in signatures note, 7C9
 more than a single letter, 0K
 of place name in source, 4B5
 of supplied name of country, etc., in publication, etc., area, 4B4
 see also Initials
Academic degrees, honors, etc., omitted from statement of responsibility, 1G8
Academic disputations
 statement(s) of responsibility for, 1G4
 see also Praeses (academic disputations); Respondent (academic disputations)
Academic dissertations, *see* Dissertations
Accents, 0H, App. B
Access point, definition, AACR 2, App. D
Access points
 serials, App. C
 titles, App. A
Accompanying material
 definition, AACR 2, App. D
 excluded from numbering in extent statement, 5B16
 general rules, 5E
 notes describing, 7C11
 option to describe such material independently or mention in note, 5E1
 option to give physical description after its name, 5E1
 separate titles, added entries for, App. A
Acronyms, *see* Initials
Adaptations, 7C2, 7C7
Added entries
 notes as justification for, 7A
 series, used for names of serials, App. C3.4
 titles, App. A
Added entry, definition, AACR 2, App. D
Added title pages
 added entries, App. A
 definition, AACR 2, App. D
 not a plate, 5B9, App. G ("plate")
Additional titles, *see* Other title information, additional titles
Additions to bibliographic description, *see* Words or phrases Address, titles of, in statement of responsibility, 1G7
Address of printer as substitute for name in source, 4B11, 4C4

D

Extent, statement of, *(continued)*
  unnumbered pages or leaves, 5B1, 5B3, 5B6, 5B8, 5B11-5B12
      within numbered sequences, 5B3
  unpaginated volumes, 5B8
Extent of item, definition, AACR 2, App. D

F

Facing title pages, 0C1-0C2
Facsimiles as illustrative matter, 5C2
Fascicle, definition, AACR 2, App. D
Fascicles, 5B16
Fictitious attribution to a person, 7C6
Fictitious publication, etc., details, 4A4, 4C5, 4D2
Fingerprint, 8
  definition, App. G
Folded leaves, 5B10
Folded sheets, *see* Folders
Folder, definition, App. G
Folders, 5B15, 5D5
Foliation (by count of leaves), *see* Extent, statement of; Pagination
Foliation (by signature), 7C9
Formal notes, 7B3
Format, 5D1, App. C1.5
  definition ("Format (Texts)"), AACR 2, App. D
  given for works created before 1801, 5D1
  option to give for works created after 1800, 5D1
  statement of, punctuation, 5A1
Forms as illustrative matter, 5C2
French folds (as separate publications), *see* Single-sheet publications
Full stop, *see* Period
Function, designations of, in added entry headings, serials, App. C1.9

G

Gaskell's formula (signatures), 7C9
Genealogical tables as illustrative matter, 5C2
Glossary, App. G
Gothic capitals, transcription of, 0H
Graphic process or technique, option to add to illustration statement, 5C1
Gregorian calendar and date(s) of publication, etc., 4D2
Guide letters, 0G

H

Half title
    added entries, App. A
    definition, AACR 2, App. D
    not a plate, App. G ("plate")
Hand-colored illustrations, 5C3
Hand coloring, 5C3, 7C18
Heading, definition, AACR 2, App. D
Headings given in "with" notes, 7C19
Headpieces not regarded as illustrations, 5C1
Height (of volume), *see* Size
Holdings, library's, 0G, 7C7, 7C18
Honor, titles of, in statement of responsibility, 1G7
Hyphen, use of
    with title proper of multivolumed works, 1B4
    with two or more dates of publication, etc., 4D7

I

i (letter), transcription of, 0H, App. A-B
"i.e.", use of
    with corrections to misprints, 0G, App. A
    with corrections to publication information, 4A4, 4B5, 4B9, 4C5, 4D2, 4E
Illumination, 7C18
Illustrated title page
    not regarded as illustration, 5C1
    not treated as a plate, 5B9, App. G ("plate")
Illustration, definition, App. G
Illustration statement, 5C
    option to add graphic process or technique, 5C1
Illustrations
    as entire or main content of work, 5C6
    colored, 5C3
    hand-colored, 5C3
    illustrated title pages not regarded as, 5C1
    in pockets, 5C7
    numbering, 5C4, 5C7
    on endpapers, 5C5
    option to disregard minor illustrations in illustration statement, 5C1
    option to specify particular types, 5C2
    typographical ornaments not regarded as, 5C1
Imperfections in copies, 0B2, 5B12, 7C18
Impression
    as edition statement, 2B2, 2D3
    as variant, App. G ("variant")
    date of, 4D2-4D3, 4E
    definition, App. G

Issue
 as edition statement, 2B2
 as variant, App. G ("variant")
 definition, App. G

J

j (letter), transcription of, 0H, App. A-B
Julian calendar and date(s) of publication, etc., 4D2

L

Labels (mounted imprints), 4A5, 7C8
Lacunae in source of information, 0B2, 0E
Language of description, 0F, 7C2
 two or more languages
  choice of language of edition statement, 2B9
  choice of language of place of publication, 4B13
  choice of language of publisher statement, 4C11
  choice of title page as chief source where t.p. is in more than one language, 0C2
  statements of responsibility, 1G10
  statements of responsibility with edition statements, 2B9
LCRI in serials cataloging, App. C1.1, C3.4
Leaf, definition, AACR 2, App. D
Leaf of plates, definition, App. G
Leaves, *see* Pagination
Leaves, double, 5B11
Leaves, folded, 5B10
Leaves, successive (title page information), 0C1-0C2
Leaves of plates, 5B9
Lettered leaves, pages, etc., 5B1
Letterpress title page as chief source of information, 0C2
Letters, early forms of, transcription, 0H, App. A-B
 guide, 0G
 initial, *see* Initials
Library of Congress policy on application of rules, 0A (note 2)
Library of Congress typographical facilities, 0F (note 3)
Library's holdings, 0G, 7C7, 7C18
Ligatures, transcription of, 0H, App. B
Limited edition, 7C7, 7C18
Lines, number of, 7C10
Lining papers containing illustrations, 5C5
Linked data, inseparably, *see* Inseparably linked data
Loose-leaf publications, 5B13

M

Mandatory notes, 7A
    "no more published" notes, 5B21, 7C8
    on accompanying material not recorded in physical description area, 7C11
    on adaptations, 7C2
    on additional titles not named on t.p., 1E2
    on advertisements, 5B5
    on authorship, 7C6
    on bibliographical description of work based on imperfect copy, 0B2, 5B12, 7C18
    on chief source of information (t.p.), 0C2-0C3
    on conjectural dates, 4D5
    on contents, 1D2, 1F6-1F7, 7C16
    on correction of printing date when recorded as publication date, 4D2
    on dated proclamations, 4D5
    on date(s) of publication, etc, 4D2-4D3, 4D5-4D6, 4D8
    on designations such as numbering in title proper, 1B4
    on dissertations, 7C13
    on double pagination, 5B6
    on duplicated sequences of paging, 5B6
    on edition and bibliographic history of item, 2B5, 7C7, 7C13
    on errata leaves, 5B4, 7C16
    on extent, 5B1, 5B4-5B6, 5B11-5B12, 5B16-5B17, 5B21, 7C10
    on guide letters for initial letters, 0G
    on hand coloring, 5C3, 7C18
    on illustrations, 5C5, 5C7
    on imperfections in copies, 0B2, 5B12
    on incunabula, 7C10, 7C14
    on inferred name of publisher, 4C4, 4C8
    on lacunae in source of information, 0B2
    on language of publication, etc., 7C2
    on leaves of a pre-1801 volume, numbered and printed on one side only, 5B1
    on lengthy statements of date of publication, 4D2
    on limited editions, 7C7
    on missing leaves or pages, 5B12
    on multipart or multivolume items, 4B7, 4C7, 4D8, 7C8
    on names of persons or bodies connected with a work, 7C6
    on number of columns, number of lines, and type measurements for incunabula, 7C10
    on numbering of pages in opposite directions, 5B6
    on numbers borne by the publication, 7C17
    on original position of transposed elements, 1B1, 1B6, 1G3, 2C2, 7C6, 7C7
    on original publication details when covered by a label or other means, 4A5
    on original titles not on t.p., 1C
    on other title information, 1D2
    on parallel titles, 1C
    on place of publication, 4B6, 4B7, 4B9-4B12
    on possible intention to separate works printed on single-sheet, 1F8
    on printer statement, 4C6
    on publication, etc., area, 4A2, 4A4-4A5

Misprints, etc., *see* Errors in item

Monograph title page as source of series information, 0D

Mottoes in title page transcription, 1A2

Multilingual items, *see* Language of description

Multipart item, definition, AACR 2, App. D

Multipart items

    extent, 5B16-5B21

    individual issues of serials, App. C3.3

    option to record date of each volume in note, 4D7

    use of contents notes, 7C16

    with changes in place of publication, 4B7

    with changes in publisher, etc., 4C7

    with continuous pagination, option to record pagination of each unit, 5B19

    with different volume heights, 5D3

    with several chief sources of information, 0C2

    with title proper including numbering, etc., 1B4

    with two or more dates of publication, etc., 4D7-4D8

    without continuous pagination, option to record pagination of each unit, 5B20

Multiscript items, *see* Script of description

Multivolumed items, *see* Multipart items

Music as illustrative matter, 5C2

N

Names of persons or bodies as title proper, 1B3

    in publication, etc., area, 4B-4C

"No more published" notes, 5B21, 7C8

Nobility, titles of, in statement of responsibility, 1G7

Non-book formats, MARC code "dcrb" not applied to, App. E

Note area

    capitalization, 7B3

    general instructions and preliminary rule, 7A-7B

    paragraphing, 7B1

    prescribed sources of information, 0D, 7B2

    punctuation, 7B1

Notes

    as justification for added entries for special files, 7A, App. A

    based on dealers' descriptions, added to minimal-level records, App. D

    bibliographic citations in, 0B2, 7B3, 7C6, 7C14, App. D

    combining two or more notes, 7C

    containing introductory words or phrases, 7B3

    containing quotations, 7B3

    copy-specific, 0G, 7C7, 7C18

    form of, 7B3

    formal, 7B3

    giving full collation instead of signatures, 7C9

    in a work, phrases about on title page, 1G14, 2C3, App. A

    informal, 7B3

Notes *(continued)*

O

P

Plate, definition, App. G

Plates, 5B9

    see also Engraved title page; Illustrated title page

Plates, double, 5B9

Plus sign, use of

    with statement of accompanying material, 5A1, 5E1

    with unknown foliation or pagination, 5B12

Pockets containing illustrative matter, 5C7, 5E2

Portfolio, definition, AACR 2, App. D

Portfolios, 5B14, 5B16

Portraits as illustrative matter, 5C2

Position or office held, omitted from statement of responsibility, 1G8

Praeses (academic disputations)

    definition, AACR 2, App. D

    in statement of responsibility, 1G4

Preliminaries

    as source of information, 0D, 1G1, 2A2, 4A2

    definition, AACR 2, App. D

Prepositions with places of publication, 4B2

Prescribed sources of information, *see* Sources of information

Price, 1A2, 8

"Printed in the year", 4D1

Printer

    as publisher, 4

    identification of, in physical description note, 7C10

    in publisher statement, 4C1-4C2, 4C6

    location of printer sometimes preferred over publisher for very early publications, 4B10

Printer statement and publisher statement in separate sources, 4C6

Printer's address as substitute for name in source, 4B11, 4C4

Printer's device, *see* Publisher's device

Printer's sign as substitute for name in source, 4B11, 4C4

Printer's usage as guide to transcription, 0H, App. B

Printing, *see* Impression

"Privately printed" statement, 4C2

Privilege statement, 7C8

Proclamations, date(s) of publication, etc., 4D5

Provenance, 7C18

Pseudonym, definition, AACR 2, App. D

Pseudonyms in statement of responsibility, 1G8

Publication, etc., area, 4

    collections, unpublished or miscellaneous, 4A6

    fictitious or incorrect information, 4A4-4A5, 4B9, 4C5

    option to give additional imprint information in note, 4A2

    option to transcribe publisher and printer statements from different sources, 4C6

    prescribed sources of information, 0D, 4A2

    punctuation, 4A1

    speculative details, 4A4

    transcribed in "with" note, 7C19

Publications, discontinued, 5B21

Q

Qualifications, academic, omitted from statement of responsibility, 1G8
Question mark, use of
    with conjectural interpolation, 0E
    with conjectural meaning of abbreviation or contraction, 0J2
    with supplied publisher where uncertain, 4C8
    with uncertain date(s) of publication, etc., 4D5-4D6
    with uncertain place of publication, 4B12
Quotations in notes, 7B3

R

r (letter), transcription of, App. B
Rare books, need for detailed description, 0A
Rare serials, *see* Serials
Reference source, definition, AACR 2, App. D
Reference sources
    for basic description, 0B2
    for contents notes, 7C16
    for date(s) of publication, etc., 4D2-4D3
    for notes, 7A, 7B3, 7C6, 7C9, 7C14, App. D
    for publication, etc., area, 4A2
"References" notes, 7C7, 7C14, App. C1.6, App. D
Reimpression, *see* Impression
Relator terms and codes, serials, App. C1.9, C2.9-C2.10
Religious orders, initials of, in statement of responsibility, 1G8
Reprint, definition, AACR 2, App. D
Respondent (academic disputations)
    definition, AACR 2, App. D
    in statement of responsibility, 1G4
Revisions, edition statements, 2D-2E
Rolls, 5B14-5B15
Roman dates, 4D2
Roman numerals
    and arabic numerals in same sequence of pagination, 5B6
    capitalization, 0H, 5B1
    changed to arabic numerals in date of publication, 4D2 erroneous or misprinted in date(s) of
        publication, etc., 4D2
    option to transcribe as they appear in date(s) of publication, etc., 4D2
    pagination, 5B1
Romanization
    definition, AACR 2, App. D
    interpolations, 0F
    option to use for title proper, 7C4
Rubrication, 7C18

Running title
    added entries, App. A
    definition, AACR 2, App. D

S

s (letter), transcription of, App. B
"s.l.," use of, 4B12
"s.n.," use of, 4C9
Samples as illustrative matter, 5C2
Script of description, 0F
    two or more scripts
        choice of script of edition statement, 2B9
        choice of script of place of publication, 4B13
        choice of script of publisher statement, 4C11
        choice of title page as chief source where t.p. is in more than one language, 0C2
        statements of responsibility, 1G10
        statements of responsibility with edition statements, 2B9
Sections of items
    punctuation between, 1A1, 1B6
    title proper in two or more parts not grammatically linked, 1B6
Semicolon, use of
    not used in edition area, 2C3
    preceding each subsequent statement of responsibility, 1A1
    preceding each subsequent statement of responsibility relating to edition, 2A1
    preceding each subsequently-named place of publication, 4A1
    preceding size in physical description area, 5A1
    with titles of parts by same person(s) or body (bodies), 1E1
Sequel, definition, AACR 2, App. D
Sequels, 7C7
Serial, definition, AACR 2, App. D
Serials, App. C
    application of MARC code "dcrb", App. E
    individual issues, App. C1.8, C3
Series added entries, used for names of serials, App. C3.4
Series, definition, AACR 2, App. D
Series area, 6, 7C12
    option to give nonessential series information in note, 7C12
    prescribed sources of information, 0D
Series title page
    as source of series information, 0D
    definition, AACR 2, App. D
Sheets, *see* Single-sheet publications
Sheets, folded, *see* Folders; Single-sheet publications
"sic", use of, 0G, App. A
Sign, printer's, as substitute for name in source, 4B11, 4C4
Sign, publisher's, as substitute for name in source, 4B11, 4C4
Sign, Tironian, treated as abbreviation, 0J2

V

v (letter), transcription of, 0H, App. A-B
Variant, definition, App. G
Various pagings or foliations, 5B6
Vignettes not regarded as illustrations, 5C1
Virgule, transcription when used as a comma, 0E
Volume, definition, AACR 2, App. D
Volumes, number of, 1A2, 1D3, 5B13, 5B16-5B21

W

w (letter), transcription of, 0H, App. B
Width (of volume), *see* Size
"With" notes, 7C19
    on single-sheet publications, 1F8
    option to include issue or binding information at end of note, 7C19
    prescribed punctuation used, 7B1
"With, on verso" notes, 1F7
Woodcuts, 5C1, 7C10
Words or phrases
    as supplied title, 1A2, 1B5, 1E2
    denoting place names, in statement of responsibility, 1G8
    explanatory
        option to add to statement of responsibility, 1G9
        with edition statement, 2B1, 2B4
        with place of publication, 4B3-4B5
        with publisher statement, 4C6
    in notes, use of modern punctuation, 7B1
    in single-sheet publications, 1F2-1F4, 1F7
    introductory, in formal notes, 7B3
    noun or noun phrases, 1G11
    on t.p. notes, appendices, etc., in work, 1G14, App. A
    option to devise title for collection without meaningful title, 1E2
    option to transcribe as they appear in date of publication, 4D1
    with name of principal place of publication, 4B2
    with statements of responsibility, 1G7-1G9, 1G11
Works created after 1800
    option to count blank leaves at beginning and end, 5B3
    option to give format, 5D1
    rules for cataloging at LC, 0A (note 2)
Works created before 1801
    counting blank leaves at beginning and end, 5B3
    format, 5D1
    noting leaves numbered and printed on one side only, 5B1
    rules for cataloging at LC, 0A (note 2)